Big Data and Analytics Applications in Government

Data Analytics Applications

Series Editor: Jay Liebowitz

Big Data and Analytics Applications in Government

Current Practices and Future Opportunities

Edited by
Gregory Richards

CRC Press
Taylor & Francis Group
Boca Raton London New York

CRC Press is an imprint of the
Taylor & Francis Group, an **informa** business
AN AUERBACH BOOK

CRC Press
Taylor & Francis Group
6000 Broken Sound Parkway NW, Suite 300
Boca Raton, FL 33487-2742

© 2018 by Taylor & Francis Group, LLC
CRC Press is an imprint of Taylor & Francis Group, an Informa business

No claim to original U.S. Government works

Printed on acid-free paper

International Standard Book Number-13: 978-1-4987-6434-6 (Hardback)

Visit the Taylor & Francis Web site at
http://www.taylorandfrancis.com

and the CRC Press Web site at
http://www.crcpress.com

Contents

Preface

Why Government Analytics? Why Now?

Editor's Introduction to This Volume

The Big Data phenomenon started out of necessity because of the large amounts of data generated by the Internet companies (primarily Yahoo and Google). These organizations needed to find a way to manage data continually generated by users of their search engines and so in 2004, Jeffrey Dean and Sanjay Ghemawat of Google released a paper in which they described techniques for distributed processing of large data sets. Since then, the field has grown in several directions: newer technologies that improve data capture, transformation, and dissemination have been invented as has new techniques for analyzing and generating insights. In addition, new structural models in organizations, for example, the creation of chief data officers, are being adopted to better manage data as a corporate asset.

In contrast, *analytics* has long been a staple of public sector organizations. Scientists working in fields such as space engineering, protection of waterways, prediction of the impact of policies, or in gathering and analyzing demographic information have for many years relied on statistical techniques to improve decision-making. Practical examples such as the United States Federal Drug Administration use of analytics for adopting a risk-based approach to inspecting manufacturing facilities, the Bureau of Indian Affairs Crime Analytics program, the use of advanced statistics in many countries for enhanced border control, and the continued growth of Compstat-style approaches pioneered in New York City attest to the widespread adoption of analytics programs within the public sector.

In many cases, however, these examples are *point* solutions focused on one specific area within an organization. The Big Data phenomenon has encouraged a democratization of analytics across organizations as managers learn that analytic techniques can be applied outside of strict scientific or financial contexts to improve program delivery. It is for this reason I used the term Big Data Analytics (BDA). Some analytic techniques require large data sets, but others use smaller data sets to deliver insights to program managers. In each case, it is the application of analytic techniques to data that helps to improve program delivery, not the fact that the data exists.

With these observations in mind, the first question: *why government analytics?* can be answered by noting that government organizations are no different to any other organization when it comes to ensuring the delivery of value for money. Managers and politicians alike seek to do the best they can often do with limited budgets working in an environment characterized by rapidly changing external conditions. Where government organizations differ from those in the private sector is in the level of complexity and ambiguity that is part and parcel of managing in public sector organizations. Within this context, BDA can be an important tool given that many analytic techniques within the Big Data world have been created specifically to deal with complexity and rapidly changing conditions. The important task for public sector organizations is to liberate analytics from narrow scientific silos and expand it across the organization to reap maximum benefit across the portfolio of programs.

The second question: *why now?* can be answered by realizing that up until a few years ago, a significant amount of attention was focused on simply being able to gather and process data. The tools are now available to do so. We need to turn our attention to the *application* of analytics to derive insight and drive program efficiency. To apply BDA effectively, three factors are important. First, the data should be available and accessible to users. Second, analysts and managers need to understand how to process and draw insights from the data.

Third, a context for the use of BDA needs to exist. Some researchers refer to this context as a *data-driven* culture: that is, an organization whose management team relies on evidence for decision-making and overall management.

Few public sector organizations have all three factors in place. Accordingly, this volume highlights contextual factors important to better situating the use of BDA within organizations and demonstrates the wide range of applications of different BDA techniques. The first chapter by Matthew Chegus, *Big Data and Analytics in Government Organizations: A Knowledge-Based Perspective* argues that BDA is in fact a knowledge-generating mechanism, and organizations should be aware that without a means to manage knowledge well, BDA initiatives are likely to fail. Chapter 2, *Setting the Context for Analytics: Performance Management in Canadian Public Organizations: Findings of a Multi-Case Study* and Chapter 3, *Preparing for Analytics: The Dubai Government Excellence Program* provide an overview of how public sector organizations in Canada and Dubai are organizing to better manage performance. These chapters highlight the importance of leadership and organizational practices that lead to good performance. The point being that BDA initiatives should not be *bolted on*: they should be integrated into the organization's performance management processes.

Chapters 4 through 10 provide examples of different applications of BDA in public sector organizations. Chapter 4, *Leveraging Innovation Systems: Supporting Science and Technology Capability Analysis through Big Messy Data Visualization* explores the use of tools that visualize science and technology capability in such a way as to enable managers to make informed decisions about improvement initiatives. Chapter 5, *Big Data Analytics and Public Bus Transportation Systems in China: A strategic Intelligence Approach Based on Knowledge and Risk Management,* discusses the use of sensor data to enable hybrid buses to run on time while minimizing the use of fossil fuels to the extent possible. Chapter 6, *Government of India prepares for Big Data Analytics Using Aadhaar Card Unique Identification System* provides an overview of the considerable amount of work that needed to be done on the data supply chain to implement India's Aadhaar card. Chapter 7, *Visual Data Mining with Virtual Reality Spaces: Exploring Canadian Federal Government Data* outlines a useful approach for visualizing heterogenous data. Chapter 8, *Institutionalizing Analytics: A Case Study* demonstrates the holistic approach taken by one organization to integrate analytics into its day-to-day operations. The important point about this chapter is that leaders in this organization anticipated that the use of analytics would lead to change and therefore they adopted a process that recognized the complexity of change management in a public sector context. Chapter 9, *Modeling Data Sources*, defines the use of a goal-mapping software to link business objectives to tasks and ultimately to data sources. The point of this approach is to enable managers to better understand whether data are indeed available for decision-making and how to adapt information systems in the face of changing organizational priorities. Chapter 10, *Analyzing Predictors of Severe Traffic Accidents* demonstrates the use of the *Cross-Industry Standard Process for Data Mining* (CRISP-DM) at the municipal level to explore factors that might enable police forces to predict where and when severe traffic accidents are likely to occur. The analysis is important but more so is the structured process (i.e., CRISP-DM) used to generate findings about the data set itself and the likely factors that influence severe accidents.

There are other examples of BDA in public sector organizations, many of them are related to public safety, and so detailed reports suitable for inclusion in this volume were not available. Those chapters selected are meant to highlight the diversity of factors that need to be managed to launch and sustain BDA initiatives in public sector organizations.

Gregory Richards
University of Ottawa

Editor

Gregory Richards holds an MBA and a PhD in business management with an emphasis on knowledge management in organizations. He worked within the Canadian federal government for a period of 5 years before moving onto Cognos Incorporated, Ottawa, Canada, as Director of Market Development. His work at the University of Ottawa, Ottawa, Canada, was stimulated by his work at Cognos: to explore the ways in which organizations use data to improve performance. He is currently a director of the Centre for Business Analytics and Performance as well as the Public Sector Performance Management research cluster and the MBA program at the University of Ottawa. He works closely with several public sector organizations that are particularly related to the applications of analytic techniques.

Contributors

Okhaide Akhigbe
School of Electrical Engineering
  and Computer Science
University of Ottawa
Ottawa, Ontario, Canada

Daniel Amyot
School of Electrical Engineering
  and Computer Science
University of Ottawa
Ottawa, Ontario, Canada

Matthew Chegus
Telfer School of Management
University of Ottawa
Ottawa, Ontario, Canada

Catherine Elliott
Telfer School of Management
University of Ottawa
Ottawa, Ontario, Canada

Sean Geddes
Telfer School of Management
University of Ottawa
Ottawa, Ontario, Canada

Gary Geling
Defence Research and
  Development Canada
Ottawa, Ontario, Canada

Swee C. Goh
Telfer School of Management
University of Ottawa
Ottawa, Ontario, Canada

Khaled Khattab
Government of Dubai
United Arab Emirates

Kevin Lai
Telfer School of Management
University of Ottawa
Ottawa, Ontario, Canada

Anthony J. Masys
Defence Research and
    Development Canada
Ottawa, Ontario, Canada

Gregory Richards
Telfer School of Management
University of Ottawa
Ottawa, Ontario, Canada

Eduardo Rodriguez
University of Ottawa
Ottawa, Ontario, Canada
and Harrisburg University
Harrisburg, Pennsylvania

Rajesh K. Tyagi
HEC Montréal
Montréal, Québec, Canada

Julio J. Valdes
National Research Council
Ottawa, Ontario, Canada

Andrew Vallerand
Defence Research and
    Development Canada
Ottawa, Ontario, Canada

Nikhil Varma
Anisfield School of Business
Ramapo College
Mahwah, New Jersey

PART I
CONCEPTUAL

1

Big Data and Analytics in Government Organizations

A Knowledge-Based Perspective

MATTHEW CHEGUS

Contents

Introduction

Big Data Analytics (BDA) has been a popular topic in the private sector for some time. However, less is understood about its application in the public sector. With increasingly knowledge-based services dominating the economy, the cultivation and deployment of various forms of knowledge and the tools that enable it are critical for any organization seeking to perform well (Chong, Salleh, Noh Syed Ahmad, & Syed Omar Sharifuddin, 2011; Harvey, Skelcher, Spencer, Jas, & Walshe, 2010; Rashman, Withers, & Hartley, 2009; Richards & Duxbury, 2015). Private firms often acknowledge the impact of organizational knowledge on innovation and firm performance (Walker, Brewer, Boyne, & Avellaneda, 2011). Yet, findings related to knowledge management (KM) in public-sector organizations have been somewhat mixed (Choi & Chandler, 2015; Kennedy & Burford, 2013; Massingham, 2014; Rashman et al., 2009). Some draw parallels between private and public organizations, where both maybe delivering some type of service (Choi & Chandler, 2015), whereas others caution that the application of private-sector organizational knowledge frameworks to public bodies might be untenable due to the differences in organizational environments such as ownership and control (Pokharel & Hult, 2010; Rashman et al., 2009; Riege & Lindsay, 2006; Willem & Buelens, 2007).

Furthermore, just as theoretical insights differ, the use of technologies and tools differs between public and private organizations. It has been argued that BDA initiatives in public-sector organizations are generally underutilized and the value returned is less than expected (Kim, Trimi, & Chung, 2014). Conflicting goals, changing leadership, stewardship of values, and challenges in measuring outcomes are all thought to constrain the use of BDA in public organizations (Joseph & Johnson, 2013; Kim et al., 2014; Washington, 2014).

Ultimately, public-sector organizations serve the people, and it is this ideological orientation and the ensuing stakeholder relationships that determine the appropriate use of BDA and delineate the differences in application from the private sector (Riege & Lindsay, 2006; Walker et al., 2011). The processes associated with BDA can be used to effectively manage knowledge and thus produce better program outcomes if employed not just to collect and store data but also to learn from these data to create meaning and insight. This article, therefore, is an exploration of the current literature on organizational knowledge and its related fields such as organizational learning (OL), in an effort to develop a conceptual framework for the successful application of BDA in the public sector. To do so, a literature review on KM, OL, and BDA was conducted to identify current thinking related to the public-sector context. This document briefly defines the literature search, explores concepts of knowledge as it relates to public-sector organizational conceptual framework, and then discusses the framework developed based on the findings from the literature review. A series of propositions based on the conceptual framework is then provided.

Literature Search

A systematic literature search was conducted in combination with more directed literature reviews. We started with seminal works in KM to provide initial direction and insight and then conducted multiple searches of the recent literature through the Web of Science citation database and ABI/INFORM Global with key words relating to KM, OL, information technology (IT), and BDA. Three questions drove the search for current literature pertinent to a discussion on KM and BDA in the public sector: What are the key elements of effective KM in the public sector? What differentiates use of BDA in public organizations from that in private firms? How can public-sector organizations effectively manage knowledge supported by BDA? The initial searches, along with their search terms and findings, are described in the appendix.

Managing Knowledge: Organizational Knowledge and Learning

To better define a conceptual framework for BDA, it makes sense to first address the concept of organizational knowledge and learning. The use of knowledge in the organization is generally related to helping individuals and organizations learn, and the hierarchy of data, information, and knowledge is a well-discussed notion. However, the literature review suggests that the strict separation between data, information, and knowledge might not, in fact, be entirely appropriate to the ways in which organizations use knowledge.

Authors such as Polanyi, Dewey, Penrose, and Hayek have contributed to different theoretical perspectives of knowledge (Rashman et al., 2009). Nonaka and Takeuchi (1995), Tsoukas and Vladimirou (2001), and others have extended such insights by exploring conceptual models of knowledge within organizations. A core theme, discussed extensively by Nonaka and Takeuchi (1995), is the distinction between tacit and explicit forms of knowledge. Within this conceptualization, data would be considered explicit: it describes the specific circumstances of the moment and so maybe more easily measured and recorded through concrete means. From a constructivist perspective, knowledge, being inherently more generalized, is more abstract and subject to all manner of individual perception. However, Nonaka and Takeuchi argue that such distinctions between explicit and tacit knowledge maybe a false dichotomy; the more generalized form may not exist without the specifics from which those generalized patterns were abstracted.

Data may thus be seen as the lowest level of *informational units* comprising an ordered sequence of items that becomes *information* when the units are organized in some context-based format. That is, information emerges when data items are generalized from a specific context such as an organizational problem or opportunity. Knowledge has been represented as the ability to draw distinctions and judgments based on an appreciation of context, theory, or both (Tsoukas & Vladimirou, 2001). More particularly, organizational knowledge would be created through a process of cognitive assimilation where decision makers consider information abstracted from a specific context (Richards & Duxbury, 2015), leading to an understanding of the current situation and the organizational response required (Tsoukas & Vladimirou, 2001).

The putative relationship between data, information, and knowledge appears to be that knowledge is built upon contextualized information units lower in the hierarchy. That is, the knowledge creation process is sequential, starting with data as its lowest level. At each subsequent level, individuals attempt to generalize in order to gain context-specific insight. This process of generalization is helpful as it allows information to be utilized in many more circumstances, patterns to be seen between divergent applications, and lessons to be learned from a variety of experiences. However, generalization may also be problematic. Generalization from specifics may seem relatively straightforward, but such conclusions maybe difficult to apply to other specific circumstances if overgeneralized or oversimplified, or otherwise, inappropriate inferences are made. Tsoukas and Vladimirou (2001) caution that individuals understand generalizations only through connecting them to particular circumstances. Fowler and Pryke (2003) raise a similar alarm, noting that, as discussed previously, knowledge is not just objective information but also the perception arising through each persons' experiences. Thus, a tension maybe seen between the specific form of information (data) and the more generalized form of information (knowledge) that gives credence to the notion that there is some kind of information flow between apparently distinct categories of knowledge.

This paper not only recognizes that different forms of knowledge are related but also supports Nonaka and Takeuchi's idea that such distinctions maybe false dichotomies. Specifically, this paper asserts that the only meaningful distinction between data, information, and knowledge is the level of generalization. The current notions of explicit knowledge exist as observable artifacts (such as a direct empirical measurement), whereas tacit knowledge is generated through the abstract process of cognitive assimilation. This reasoning leads to the model shown in Figure 1.1, where dimensions of knowledge range from low level (data) to high level (knowledge). However, how one may abstract knowledge from data is the resulting question of this assertion.

Pokharel and Hult (2010) describe learning as acquiring and interpreting information to create meaning. Indeed, other authors share similar sentiments. Barette, Lemyre, Corneil, and Beauregard (2012) described different schools of thought from cognitive-based learning to social constructivist learning; the former is characterized as changes in information based on reflections of individuals, whereas the latter is more the result of multiple people sharing their specific experiences and extracting commonalities. All three perspectives relate specifics to generalities through some sort of process or transformation indicative of Richards and Duxbury's *assimilation*. Barette et al. (2012) reflect this notion by saying "Knowledge management and OL models overlap in terms of common fundamental concepts related to learning" (p. 138). Fowler and Pryke (2003), Chawla and

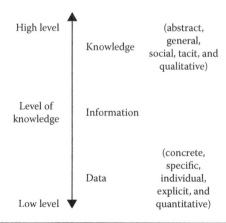

Figure 1.1 Dimensions of knowledge.

Joshi (2011), Kennedy and Burford (2013), and Harvey et al. (2010) echo similar observations. Learning, therefore, maybe considered the process by which information is generalized and abstracted to produce knowledge transitioning from lower levels of data to higher levels of knowledge.

As individuals undergoing this process would be relying on their previously acquired information, the process of learning would necessarily be influenced by all the previously acquired information, making learning a highly subjective affair. What one might recognize as a pattern might only be so because of previous patterns observed, for example. This would imply that learning is highly path-dependent, tacit, and idiosyncratic: "knowledge is not just objective information, but also is as much about the perception arising when information is refracted through the individual's personal lens" (Fowler & Pryke, 2003). These learning idiosyncrasies support the existing notions of the subjectivity of knowledge such as in the social constructivist view.

The Public-Sector Context

A number of common themes appear in the literature that describe the differences between private- and public-sector organizations: political influence being a significant contributor to organizational decision making (Barette et al., 2012; Pokharel & Hult, 2010; Rashman et al., 2009; Willem & Buelens, 2007), differences in power and control structures (Pokharel & Hult, 2010; Rashman et al., 2009; Willem & Buelens, 2007), accountability and transparency (Barette et al., 2012; Choi & Chandler, 2015; Greiling & Halachmi, 2013; Pokharel & Hult, 2010; Rashman et al., 2009), non-market not-for-profit orientation (Barette et al., 2012; Choi & Chandler, 2015; Rashman et al., 2009; Riege & Lindsay, 2006; Walker et al., 2011), public organizations motivated by stakeholder versus shareholder priorities in private organizations (Cong & Pandya, 2003; Rashman et al., 2009; Riege & Lindsay, 2006), constraints on organizational structure (Choi & Chandler, 2015; Pokharel & Hult, 2010), organizational fragmentation (Barette et al., 2012), and ambiguity of goals (Choi & Chandler, 2015; Willem & Buelens, 2007). These differences between private and public organizations lend credence to the notion that public organizations are, on a fundamental level, subject to different influences than private organizations, and therefore, the process of learning and knowledge creation might also differ.

However, there are also some similarities that draw attention (Choi & Chandler, 2015). Both private- and public-sector organizations deliver services, for example, that would seem to be a point of commonality. Willem and Buelens (2007) argue that publicness is not, in fact, a dichotomy: government institutions (i.e., public administration, taxation, and national defense), public-sector institutions (i.e., schools and hospitals), and state enterprises, all may have varying degrees of *publicness*. Attributes such as ownership, funding, control, interests, access to facilities, and agency are qualities that may influence the degree to which an organization is public or private (p. 584), as Figure 1.2 depicts.

With this continuum of publicness in mind, New Public Management (NPM) attempts to take the notion of similarities between private- and public-organizational outcomes one step further by assuming that public organizations can and should benefit from private-sector methodologies that emphasize market orientation over traditional notions of public management (Cong & Pandya, 2003; Walker et al., 2011). Such an orientation suggests that managing performance in the public sector should follow from private organizations. Essentially, NPM provides a test for the underlying notions of similarities and differences between organizational sectors, and it was tested by Walker et al. (2011). The authors found for public organizations that market orientation has the opposite effect for private and public organizations (p. 715). Just because both sectors provide services to customers does not mean that they are motivated by, perform in similar ways to, or are evaluated against the same ideals.

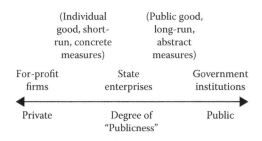

Figure 1.2 Degree of publicness.

Public- and private-sector organizations may face similar tasks. They may even produce similar outcomes and exist on a spectrum between private and public. However, fundamental differences in how these organizations perform, what drives their structures and decision making, and how they are judged to be successful suggest significant differences between private and public organizations. Such differences are large enough that the underlying assumptions of concepts like NPM should be put into question. A more general point that has started to emerge from this particular topic is the notion of a time horizon. Choi and Chandler's (2015) characterization of "myopic evaluation" (p. 144) implies an inappropriately short time horizon, which may not be comparable between sectors. Indeed, although one can argue that any organization that wishes continual existence should be concerned with long-run challenges, emphasis of private sector on quarterly results does not always reflect such a priority. With an assumption that a democratic system's public organizations exist to serve the public, especially in cases where the public good is best served by looking beyond the horizon of a single time period, much longer time horizons should be considered for all aspects of public organizations. The implication this has for KM is that public organizations tend to deal with higher levels of information and knowledge compared with private organizations because of their long-run outlook and broader scales of concern for the public good.

Consequently, not only the above-mentioned notions of dimensions of knowledge and publicness can be combined together, but also different organizational models maybe mapped to such a landscape. This landscape shows that private organizations tend to deal with lower levels of knowledge, are shorter in time horizon, and deal with more concrete measures of performance and accountability. By contrast, public organizations tend to deal with higher levels of knowledge, where more people are involved; time horizons are longer; and measures of performance and accountability are more abstract and difficult to define and measure. It must also be recognized that each organizational archetype would have many varieties, and so, there maybe examples of private organizations that deal with high-level knowledge and examples of public organizations that deal with low-level knowledge. For example, a corporate-planning exercise for a private multinational organization would necessarily include broader consideration

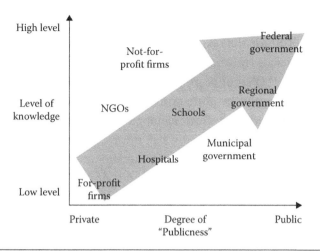

Figure 1.3 Conceptual framework-degree of publicness versus dimensions of knowledge.

than just a single individual's goals or just the next quarter's financial results, just as a municipal government maybe more concerned with local and immediate operational concerns, such as local infrastructure, whereas a federal government would be more concerned with long-term welfare of the entire population. Such propositions are reasonable from a level of analysis point of view; the grander the scale of people, time, and resources, the more general the inputs and outputs of those organizations, as measured by these qualities. Federal governments, for example, discuss ideological questions that explore how to best organize the country, whereas private firms discuss operational questions of how to exploit knowledge and resources for personal gain. Figure 1.3 provides the conceptual framework that maps the two dimensions of knowledge and publicness and places different types of organizations in relative position to each other.

The Role of Big Data and Analytics

Based on the conceptual framework, we can now explore the role of BDA within the knowledge-generating processes of public-sector organizations. Dixon, McGowan, and Cravens (2009) highlight the use of technology for KM in a public organization in two ways: to capture and to share knowledge (p. 256). Whereas data or information capture and dissemination maybe easily achieved, more abstract knowledge activities maybe more difficult. Advocates of technology in KM describe a *coming of age* (Butler, Feller, Pope, Emerson, & Murphy, 2008) for the use of technology in knowledge creation and storage, retrieval, transfer, application, and administration (p. 262). O'Malley's (2014) account of a public-sector organization's adoption of Big Data seems to be quite positive based on its impact on performance: "we moved away from ideological, hierarchical, bureaucratic governing, and we moved toward information age governing-an administrative approach that is fundamentally entrepreneurial, collaborative, interactive, and performance driven" (p. 555). However, such a description seems to imply more data- and information-based processes that deal with the explicit component of knowledge.

Riemenschneider, Allen, Armstrong, and Reid (2010) argue that this situation might exist because decisions about technology in public-sector organizations are often crisis-driven and long-term planning is limited by political cycles. Accordingly, the focus of technology-based KM tools has often been on lower-level data capture and storage. Fowler and Pryke (2003) also note that the civil service is too narrowly focused on the management of explicit information. One might extrapolate this pattern of *data centrism* to conclude that most technological tools used in KM tend, particularly in the public sector, tend to deal well with data and information, as these informational units are more explicit and so more easily captured by IT systems. The abstract characteristics associated with knowledge mean that it is not as easily represented in these systems.

Kim et al. (2014) classify most current governmental applications of Big Data as at an early stage of development and are merely large traditional data sets that do not exploit the full potential of Big Data (p. 84). This is consistent with the development of analytic capabilities in organizations, which often begins with a data-centric approach such as investments in technology that help with the capture, storage, and transmission of information (Chen, Chiang, & Storey, 2012; Holsapple, Lee-Post, & Pakath, 2014). Moving beyond the data-processing stage, organizations start to derive benefits from data as they learn to better link their data sources to organizational context to create information and eventually knowledge. Context, as discussed previously, has unique characteristics in public-sector organizations. Going beyond simply capturing information, Joseph and Johnson (2013) describe the different types of analytics possible, such as descriptive, predictive, and prescriptive analytics (p. 43), which can aid public organizations in the process of learning from data through reducing data complexity via generalization that provides a platform on which knowledge can be based.

Theorizing the Use of Big Data and Analytics in Public-Sector Organizations

The concepts discussed herein regarding KM, OL, and BDA in the public sector maybe summarized as follows. Knowledge maybe thought of as *levels of knowledge;* it begins at the lowest level of data and is abstracted or generalized through a process of learning to ever-higher levels of knowledge in a hierarchy where the former is the foundation for the latter. Low levels of knowledge are easily dealt with by IT tools, because they are more explicit and codifiable. High levels require more context and qualitative understanding in order to make sense of and use of such knowledge. These relationships constitute a dimension of knowledge.

Organizations may also be described along a dimension of *publicness*. Low-publicness (private) organizations have more individualistically defined scope based on a narrowed set of shareholders and often a shorter time horizon operating around more narrowly defined, and explicit, concepts of operational success. Highly public organizations, on the other hand, by definition, have broader scope based on the entirety of the public body that they represent and consequently have larger time horizons. Moreover, due to the conceptual and ideological nature of the highest levels of government, they have more abstract notions of success. Because of these differences, organizations that score higher along the publicness dimension will tend to operate on higher levels of knowledge as well. Higher levels of knowledge would thus require higher levels of learning from underlying data and sharing of that knowledge throughout the organization and so should act as a significant moderator for KM activities, including the technology used. Organizational learning's influence on the outcomes of organizational technology is partially supported by existing literature (Bhatt & Grover, 2005; Real, Leal, & Roldán, 2006; Tippins & Sohi, 2003), albeit from the private sector, suggesting that such a relationship maybe even stronger for public organizations.

From this high-level overview of the relationships between knowledge, learning, and organizational types, the following hypotheses are presented:

> **Proposition 1**: *Higher publicness requires higher levels of organizational knowledge.*
>
> **Proposition 2**: *The effectiveness of Big Data and Analytics in organizations that are highly public will be mediated by the level of organizational learning practiced in the organization.*
>
> **Proposition 3**: *The degree to which organizational learning mediates the effectiveness of Big Data and Analytics that are highly public will scale with the degree to which that organization scores higher on the level of knowledge dimension.*
>
> **Proposition 4**: *Big Data and Analytics will deliver more value in highly public organizations when combined with methods that enable reductions in data complexity, such as summarizations and visualizations, to enable rapid and effective high-level knowledge outputs.*
>
> **Proposition 5**: *Big Data and Analytics will perform best in organizations that are highly public, when combined with other technologies and management practices that enable and encourage the rapid and continual sharing of organizational knowledge, particularly across organizational barriers.*

Discussion

Based on empirical research and the understanding afforded by convergent theoretical notions of OL and KM, the successful application of BDA in the public sector is expected to leverage OL to create and share high-level organizational knowledge within and beyond organizational barriers. However, this will not be an easy task. Many have suggested that public organizations do not easily facilitate the use of technology for high-level knowledge management due to their unique stakeholder environment. Top-down policy initiatives have largely failed to promote knowledge creation in public organizations, and organizational boundaries may fragment knowledge

(Rashman et al., 2009) and become an impediment to sharing (Fowler & Pryke, 2003; Massingham, 2014). In addition, political and bureaucratic power structures are not always aligned with the creation and proliferation of knowledge in public organizations (Girard & McIntyre, 2010; Joseph & Johnson, 2013; McCurdy, 2011; Piening, 2013; Willem & Buelens, 2007). Accordingly, although knowledge should be an important part of a public organization's operations, a number of significant barriers exist.

Jennings and Hall (2012) suggest a framework for identifying those organizations willing to support data and evidence-based decisions, whereby a low-conflict setting exists and the organization employs members with high scientific and technical capacity. However, the number of public organizations lacking political conflict, let alone engaging large proportions of scientifically and technically capable members, is likely to be low. Consequently, although BDA shows potential to enhance the high-level KM capabilities of public organizations, to do so would require the explicit direction and support from the many and varied stakeholders involved. Reaching consensus on these matters will likely happen first on the lower-level dimensions of knowledge, as such matters are more operational and short-termed, where the outcomes of increased knowledge capabilities can clearly be seen and argued through a business's value proposition. On the other hand, higher knowledge-based capabilities maybe contested for some time owing to political disagreements about organizational goals and ambiguity of the value of outcomes, which may not only be abstract in nature but also play out over longer time scales than a single election cycle. Consequently, Big Data and Analytics researchers and practitioners alike will have to take into consideration that the theoretical relationships between capabilities and outcomes will be potentially influenced by many intervening variables. Whether success is attainable will depend on the leadership, culture, and organizational structure necessary to support technological and learning activities. Time will tell how quickly BDA will proliferate into public organizations, but hopefully, these technologies will continue to provide enhanced abilities for the organizations that benefit everyone.

Appendix: Literature Review Search Terms and Findings

WEB OF SCIENCE	ABI/INFORM GLOBAL
KNOWLEDGE MANAGEMENT/ORGANIZATIONAL LEARNING	
((knowledge NEAR/1 manage*) OR (organization* NEAR/1 learn*)) AND "public sector"	*((knowledge NEAR/1 manage*) OR (organization* NEAR/1 learn*)) AND "public sector"*
Limit to 2010–2016 (inclusive)	Limited to 2010–2016 (inclusive)
Search in TOPIC (title, abstract, keywords, Keywords Plus)	Search in title OR abstract
Language = English	Language = English
Document type = Article, Review, Editorial	Limit to peer-reviewed and scholarly journals
BIG DATA IN THE PUBLIC SECTOR	
(big NEAR/1 data) AND ("public sector")	*(big NEAR/1 data) AND ("public sector")*
Limit to 2010–2016 (inclusive)	Limited to 2010–2016 (inclusive)
Search in TOPIC (title, abstract, keywords, Keywords Plus)	Search in title OR abstract
Language = English	Language = English
Document type = Article, Review, Editorial	Limit to peer reviewed and scholarly journals
ABSORPTIVE CAPACITY IN THE PUBLIC SECTOR	
((absorptive NEAR/1 capacit*) AND "public sector")	*((absorptive NEAR/1 capacit*) AND "public sector")*
Limit to 2010–2016 (inclusive)	Limited to 2010–2016 (inclusive)
Search in TOPIC (title, abstract, keywords, Keywords Plus)	Search in title OR abstract
Language = English	Language = English
Document type = Article, Review, Editorial	Limit to peer-reviewed and scholarly journals

Following the searches, a chronological review of articles from leading public-sector research journals was also conducted in the *Journal of Public Administration Research and Theory* and *Public Administration Review*. Articles were considered on their basis of overlap with concepts in knowledge management in the public sector. Once duplicated results were removed, a total of 178 articles were reviewed for their pertinence and excluded if not relevant. Finally, if there were topics that were deemed important for the issues at hand but were underrepresented in the resultant literature, additional articles were considered based on a specific search for those topics. The below-mentioned chart represents both the included seminal works in knowledge management and related fields in addition to the most influential of the included search result articles that have formed the basis for the above discussion. The chart categorizes each article based on its application to the questions at hand and the contribution of each article to its respective area of study, in chronological order within each category.

ARTICLE	CONTRIBUTION
ORGANIZATIONAL KNOWLEDGE	
The knowledge creating company: How Japanese companies create the dynamics of innovation. (Nonaka & Takeuchi, 1995)	The creation of knowledge through a cycle (spiral) that is continuously changing form between tacit and explicit.
What is organizational knowledge? (Tsoukas & Vladimirou, 2001)	Individual knowledge becomes organizational knowledge through its codification and propositions underlain by collective understanding. Knowledge as the ability to draw distinctions and judgment based on context and/or theory.
Knowledge management in public service provision: The child support agency (Fowler & Pryke, 2003)	Empirically testing Nonaka and Takeuchi's model of five enabling factors for knowledge creation in a public-organization setting, finding tacit knowledge to be suboptimally managed in favor of information management.
ORGANIZATIONAL LEARNING	
How do public organizations learn? Bridging cultural and structural perspectives (Moynihan & Landuyt, 2009)	Learning as creating knowledge. Empirical test to find which variables foster organizational learning in a public organization: information systems, adequacy of resources, mission orientation, decision flexibility, and learning forums.
Organizational learning and knowledge in public service organizations: A systematic review of the literature (Rashman et al., 2009)	Data as ordered sequences of items; information as context-based arrangement of items. Organizational learning can be described as a process of individual and shared thought and action in an organizational context involving cognitive, social, behavioral, and technical elements. Social view treats learning as inseparable from social interaction. Knowledge is seen as a key component to learning, where knowledge is the content of learning.

(*Continued*)

ARTICLE	CONTRIBUTION
Varieties of organizational learning: Investigating learning in local level public sector organizations (Pokharel & Hult, 2010)	Learning involves acquiring, interpreting, and sharing information to create meaning and is a continuous process of knowledge integration. Individual learning feeds organizational learning. Public organizations may face more constraints to learning due to higher accountability expectations, increased stakeholder variety, and legal obligations in power and control structures.
Can government organizations learn and change? (McCurdy, 2011)	Public organizations that do not change tend to exploit pockets of political support that insulates them from change and perpetuates a lack of learning. Owing to this reluctance to change, most change may occur through *replacement*.
Dimensions of the learning organization in an Indian context (Awasthy & Gupta, 2012)	Test learning in a public organization with the Dimensions of the Learning Organization Questionnaire. Individual-level learning had positive effect on organizational outcomes when mediated by structural-level learning.
Organizational learning facilitators in the Canadian public sector (Barette et al., 2012)	Creation of a measurement instrument for learning in the public sector. Six main factors found are knowledge acquisition, learning support, learning culture, leadership of learning, strategic management, and the learning environment.
Accountability and organizational learning in the public sector (Greiling & Halachmi, 2013)	A narrow focus on short-term measures for accountability maybe inhibiting long-term organizational learning.
Exploration, exploitation, and public sector innovation: An organizational learning perspective for the public sector (Choi & Chandler, 2015)	Public organizations may lack appropriate feedbacks that would otherwise balance exploration and exploitation behaviors usually resulting from temporally myopic decisions.
Exploring the relationships between the learning organization and organizational performance (Pokharel & Choi, 2015)	Empirically testing seven dimensions of organizational learning in a public-sector organization. All seven dimensions showed positive relationship with performance. Organizational-level learning has a mediating effect on the relationships between individual and group-level learning and performance.

(*Continued*)

ARTICLE	CONTRIBUTION

CONTRASTING PUBLIC AND PRIVATE ORGANIZATIONS

Issues of knowledge management in the public sector (Cong & Pandya, 2003)	Public organizations differ from private ones for two main reasons: public sector is stakeholder-dependent, whereas private sector is dependent on service delivery and is not threatened by survival.
Knowledge sharing in public sector organizations: The effect of organizational characteristics on interdepartmental knowledge sharing (Willem & Buelens, 2007)	An organization may be thought of in degrees of *publicness* rather than the traditional dichotomy based on ownership, funding, control, interests, access to facilities, and agency.
Impact of knowledge management on learning organization in Indian organizations—A comparison (Chawla & Joshi, 2011)	The impact of knowledge management on learning in vision, strategy, work practices, and information flow is found to be better for public organizations.
Market orientation and public service performance: New public management gone mad? (Walker et al., 2011)	Empirically testing New Public Management assumption that market orientation improves public service performance. Market orientation generally has a positive effect on consumer satisfaction but very little effect on organizational performance, which is the opposite of what is seen in private organizations.
A comparative analysis of conceptions of knowledge and learning in general and public sector literature 2000–2009 (Kennedy & Burford, 2013)	Schools of thought of knowledge management in the public sector lag behind more general knowledge literature traditionally aimed at more private organizations. Most existing literature on knowledge management in the public sector treats knowledge as static and codifiable, whereas contemporary scholars highlight the complexity of knowledge and its embeddedness.

KNOWLEDGE MANAGEMENT

Designing a core IT artifact for knowledge management systems using participatory action research in a government and a non-government organization (Butler et al., 2008)	Advocates for tools/technologies as being vital for the execution of knowledge management. Specifically in the areas of knowledge creation and storage, retrieval/transfer/application, management, and system administration.
Knowledge sharing using codification and collaboration technologies to improve health care: Lessons from the public sector (Dixon et al., 2009)	Knowledge management is an evolutionary process that requires periodic evaluation and reflection in order to continuously improve quality.

(Continued)

ARTICLE	CONTRIBUTION
Knowledge management modeling in public sector organizations: A case study (Girard & McIntyre, 2010)	Introduces the Inukshuk model of knowledge management in the Canadian public service as each expression being unique and built upon a foundation of technology, culture, and leadership.
KM implementation in a public sector accounting organization: An empirical investigation (Chong et al., 2011)	Empirical test of a knowledge management framework in a public organization and its impact on performance. Knowledge sharing, technology, and leadership's impact on a knowledge-sharing culture are important factors.
An evaluation of knowledge management tools: Part 2—Managing knowledge flows and enablers (Massingham, 2014)	Empirical case study of knowledge management in a public organization. Highest-rated factor was knowledge preservation, and the most value was created through creating a *why context*, which gives meaning to information.

ENACTING KNOWLEDGE THROUGH CAPABILITIES

Knowledge management in the public sector: Stakeholder partnerships in the public policy development (Riege & Lindsay, 2006)	Government functions, including policy, are based heavily on socially derived knowledge, which is difficult to capture. Effectively managed stakeholder relationships and the sharing of knowledge that results are integral to good policy. Such management needs to be considered dynamic.
Absorptive capacity in a non-market environment (Harvey et al., 2010)	A public organization maybe considered a knowledge-processing and -utilization entity, where the most important asset is the knowledge that is continuously renewed and created. Absorptive capacity occurs in three stages: exploratory learning, transformative learning, and exploitative learning. Absorptive capacity can both complement and integrate existing theories of knowledge management and knowledge processing in relation to performance.
Potential absorptive capacity of state IT departments: A comparison of perceptions of CIOS and IT managers (Riemenschneider et al., 2010)	Factors that affect a government IT department's absorptive capacity are creativity, innovative, and demonstrating initiative. It is also higher in departments that share information more readily. When an external environment is perceived as hostile, perspective of these departments will be one of reaction and minimization of risk taking.

(*Continued*)

ARTICLE	CONTRIBUTION
Evidence-based practice and the use of information in state agency decision making (Jennings & Hall, 2012)	Evidence-based decision-making capabilities in public organizations vary. Proposing a model to predict when a public organization will be evidence-based or not. Two dimensions: degree of conflict and degree of scientific capacity. Low-conflict, high scientific capacity will exhibit the highest levels of evidence-based decision making.
Written versus unwritten rules: The role of rule formalization in green tape (DeHart-Davis, Chen, & Little, 2013)	Formalized rules are often associated with organizational pathologies. However, rule-making capability, if use appropriately, can also increase effectiveness by improving rule design and compliance.
Dynamic capabilities in public organizations: A literature review and research agenda (Piening, 2013)	Dynamic capabilities maybe important for public organizations, which may face high rates of change due to frequent policy shifts. Development of dynamic capabilities follows three phases: learning through experimenting, enabling experimentation processes, and the management of ongoing tensions between innovation and exploitation. Management plays a key role in the facilitation of dynamic capabilities.
Knowledge sharing: What works and what doesn't work: A critical systems thinking perspective (Massingham, 2015)	The management of knowledge sharing should focus primarily on building social structures that can diffuse and embed tacit knowledge.
Work-group knowledge acquisition in knowledge intensive public-sector organizations: An exploratory study (Richards & Duxbury, 2015)	Information is data that has been organized to create meaning. Information that is assimilated is transformed into knowledge. Absorptive capacity is a form of knowledge acquisition in the Canadian public sector. Factors that positively affect absorptive capacity in public orgs are the role of managers, knowledge applicability, and the communality of knowledge for sharing.
BIG DATA	
5 keys to business analytics program success (Boyer, Harris, Green, Frank, & Van De Vanter, 2012)	Business analytics is a part of the whole organizational strategy, which should follow the business and not lead.
Big data and transformational government (Joseph & Johnson, 2013)	Barriers to government adoption of Big Data: Analysis of unstructured data, building Big Data infrastructure, acceptance of change in a highly bureaucratic environment, and data privacy.

(*Continued*)

ARTICLE	CONTRIBUTION
A unified foundation for business analytics (Holsapple et al., 2014)	Constructs an ontology of business analytics for further study. Provides a historical overview of analytical techniques in private-business organizations. Dimensions of analytics identified as domain, orientation, and technique. A general definition of analytics is proposed as "evidence-based problem recognition and solving that happen within the context of business situations."
Big-data applications in the government sector (Kim et al., 2014)	Big Data projects in public organizations are relatively immature. Success requires an ability to integrate and analyze information through new technologies, development of supporting systems, and the ability of Big Data to support decision making through analytics. Concerns of Big Data in government: security, speed, interoperability, analytics capabilities, and lack of competent professionals. A *business analytics framework* is proposed based on six building blocks: a *movement grounded in rationale*, a *capability set* of competencies, a *transforming process*, specific activities and practices, technologies, and the decisional paradigm under which evidence is evaluated and action is taken.
Big data and information processing in organizational decision processes (Kowalczyk & Buxmann, 2014)	Results from a multiple case study are presented. Data-centric approach is taken as Big Data addresses the supply of data. The *3-V* model of Big Data is introduced based on data volume, data velocity, and data variety. Organizational decision-making processes are discussed through information-processing theory, which has the goal of reducing uncertainty and equivocality through information processing as enabled by Big Data.
Doing what works: Governing in the age of big data (O'Malley, 2014)	Big Data is essential for transparency and accountability.
Big data and U.S. public policy (Stough & McBride, 2014)	Highlights that one of the biggest concerns of Big Data is the risk to privacy.
Government information policy in the era of big data (Washington, 2014)	Highlights limits of Big Data for use in transparency when in conflict with personal privacy.

References

Awasthy, R., & Gupta, R. K. (2012). Dimensions of the learning organization in an Indian context. *International Journal of Emerging Markets, 7*(3), 222–244.

Barette, J., Lemyre, L., Corneil, W., & Beauregard, N. (2012). Organizational learning facilitators in the Canadian public sector. *International Journal of Public Administration, 35*(2), 137–149.

Bhatt, G. D., & Grover, V. (2005). Types of information technology capabilities and their role in competitive advantage: An empirical study. *Journal of Management Information Systems, 22*(2), 253–277.

Boyer, J., Harris, T., Green, B., Frank, B., & Van De Vanter, K. (2012). *5 Keys to Business Analytics Program Success.* Big Sandy, TX: MC Press.

Butler, T., Feller, J., Pope, A., Emerson, B., & Murphy, C. (2008). Designing a core IT artefact for knowledge management systems using participatory action research in a government and a non-government organisation. *The Journal of Strategic Information Systems, 17*(4), 249–267.

Chawla, D., & Joshi, H. (2011). Impact of knowledge management on learning organization in Indian organizations—A comparison. *Knowledge and Process Management, 18*(4), 266–277.

Chen, H., Chiang, R. H., & Storey, V. C. (2012). Business intelligence and analytics: From big data to big impact. *MIS Quarterly, 36*(4), 1165–1188.

Choi, T., & Chandler, S. M. (2015). Exploration, exploitation, and public sector innovation: An organizational learning perspective for the public sector. *Human Service Organizations: Management, Leadership & Governance, 39*(2), 139–151.

Chong, S. C., Salleh, K., Noh Syed Ahmad, S., & Syed Omar Sharifuddin, S. I. (2011). KM implementation in a public sector accounting organization: An empirical investigation. *Journal of Knowledge Management, 15*(3), 497–512.

Cong, X., & Pandya, K. V. (2003). Issues of knowledge management in the public sector. *Electronic Journal of Knowledge Management, 1*(2), 25–33.

DeHart-Davis, L., Chen, J., & Little, T. D. (2013). Written versus unwritten rules: The role of rule formalization in green tape. *International Public Management Journal, 16*(3), 331–356.

Dixon, B. E., McGowan, J. J., & Cravens, G. D. (2009). Knowledge sharing using codification and collaboration technologies to improve health care: Lessons from the public sector. *Knowledge Management Research & Practice, 7*(3), 249–259.

Fowler, A., & Pryke, J. (2003). Knowledge management in public service provision: The child support agency. *International Journal of Service Industry Management, 14*(3), 254–283.

Girard, J. P., & McIntyre, S. (2010). Knowledge management modeling in public sector organizations: A case study. *International Journal of Public Sector Management, 23*(1), 71–77.

Greiling, D., & Halachmi, A. (2013). Accountability and organizational learning in the public sector. *Public Performance & Management Review*, 36(3), 380–406.

Harvey, G., Skelcher, C., Spencer, E., Jas, P., & Walshe, K. (2010). Absorptive capacity in a non-market environment: A knowledge-based approach to analysing the performance of sector organizations. *Public Management Review*, 12(1), 77–97.

Holsapple, C., Lee-Post, A., & Pakath, R. (2014). A unified foundation for business analytics. *Decision Support Systems*, 64, 130–141.

Jennings, E. T., & Hall, J. L. (2012). Evidence-based practice and the use of information in state agency decision making. *Journal of Public Administration Research and Theory*, 22(2), 245–266.

Joseph, R. C., & Johnson, N. A. (2013). Big data and transformational government. *IT Professional*, 15(6), 43–48.

Kennedy, M., & Burford, S. (2013). A comparative analysis of conceptions of knowledge and learning in general and public sector literature 2000–2009. *International Journal of Public Administration*, 36(3), 155–167.

Kim, G. H., Trimi, S., & Chung, J. H. (2014). Big-data applications in the government sector. *Communications of the ACM*, 57(3), 78–85.

Kowalczyk, D. W. I. M., & Buxmann, P. (2014). Big data and information processing in organizational decision processes. *Business & Information Systems Engineering*, 6(5), 267–278.

Massingham, P. (2014). An evaluation of knowledge management tools: Part 2–managing knowledge flows and enablers. *Journal of Knowledge Management*, 18(6), 1101–1126.

Massingham, P. (2015). Knowledge sharing: What works and what doesn't work: A critical systems thinking perspective. *Systemic Practice and Action Research*, 28(3), 197–228.

McCurdy, H. E. (2011). Can government organizations learn and change? *Public Administration Review*, 71(2), 316–319.

Moynihan, D. P., & Landuyt, N. (2009). How do public organizations learn? Bridging cultural and structural perspectives. *Public Administration Review*, 69(6), 1097–1105.

Nonaka, I., & Takeuchi, H. (1995). *The Knowledge-Creating Company: How Japanese Companies Create the Dynamics of Innovation.* New York, NY: Oxford University Press.

O'Malley, M. (2014). Doing what works: Governing in the age of big data. *Public Administration Review*, 74(5), 555–556.

Piening, E. P. (2013). Dynamic capabilities in public organizations: A literature review and research agenda. *Public Management Review*, 15(2), 209–245.

Pokharel, M. P., & Choi, S. O. (2015). Exploring the relationships between the learning organization and organizational performance. *Management Research Review*, 38(2), 126–148.

Pokharel, M. P., & Hult, K. M. (2010). Varieties of organizational learning: Investigating learning in local level public sector organizations. *Journal of Workplace Learning*, 22(4), 249–270.

Rashman, L., Withers, E., & Hartley, J. (2009). Organizational learning and knowledge in public service organizations: A systematic review of the literature. *International Journal of Management Reviews*, 11(4), 463–494.

Real, J. C., Leal, A., & Roldán, J. L. (2006). Information technology as a determinant of organizational learning and technological distinctive competencies. *Industrial Marketing Management*, 35(4), 505–521.

Richards, G. S., & Duxbury, L. (2015). Work-group knowledge acquisition in knowledge intensive public-sector organizations: An exploratory study. *Journal of Public Administration Research and Theory*, 25(4), 1247–1277.

Riege, A., & Lindsay, N. (2006). Knowledge management in the public sector: Stakeholder partnerships in the public policy development. *Journal of Knowledge Management*, 10(3), 24–39.

Riemenschneider, C. K., Allen, M. W., Armstrong, D. J., & Reid, M. F. (2010). Potential absorptive capacity of state IT departments: A comparison of perceptions of CIOs and IT managers. *Journal of Organizational Computing and Electronic Commerce*, 20(1), 68–90.

Stough, R., & McBride, D. (2014). Big data and US public policy. *Review of Policy Research*, 31(4), 339–342.

Tippins, M. J., & Sohi, R. S. (2003). IT competency and firm performance: Is organizational learning a missing link? *Strategic Management Journal*, 24(8), 745–761.

Tsoukas, H., & Vladimirou, E. (2001). What is organizational knowledge? *Journal of Management Studies*, 38(7), 973–993.

Walker, R. M., Brewer, G. A., Boyne, G. A., & Avellaneda, C. N. (2011). Market orientation and public service performance: New Public Management gone mad? *Public Administration Review*, 71(5), 707–717.

Washington, A. L. (2014). Government information policy in the era of big data. *Review of Policy Research*, 31(4), 319–325.

Willem, A., & Buelens, M. (2007). Knowledge sharing in public sector organizations: The effect of organizational characteristics on interdepartmental knowledge sharing. *Journal of Public Administration Research and Theory*, 17(4), 581–606.

PART II

SETTING THE STAGE FOR ANALYTICS
The Organizational Perspective

2

SETTING THE CONTEXT FOR ANALYTICS

Performance Management in Canadian Public Organizations: Findings of a Multi-Case Study

SWEE C. GOH, CATHERINE ELLIOTT, AND GREGORY RICHARDS

Contents

Introduction

Despite the widespread use of performance management (PM) in public-sector organizations worldwide, there has been criticism of its efficacy in fostering performance improvement. In a recent review of 30 years of public-sector PM literature, Jackson (2011) suggests that we still do not have clear answers to important questions such as: does performance measurement result in better decisions and improved outcomes? In a similar vein, Sanger (2008), in a study of local and state governments in the United States, suggests that there are still obstacles to the effective implementation of PM, such as suppressing and manipulating negative data, leading to the perception that there is a lack of transparency in the public reporting of performance. This is not surprising, as increasing pressures for accountability are forcing public-sector managers to gather metrics to justify their programs. However, as Thomas (2007) has observed, there are few incentives to recognize problems, learn from mistakes, and experiment with new strategies for improvement. A study by Radnor and McGuire (2003) illustrates this problem in the United Kingdom. The authors concluded that despite the implementation of a PM system, including balanced scorecards, there was lack of ownership and accountability for the system, and most managers were *working the system* to meet externally imposed requirements for reporting on performance.

Beyond the conceptual, philosophical, and value interpretations of PM in the public sector, an increasing amount of empirical work has been undertaken to better understand the benefits (Kelman, 2006), impacts (Wichowsky & Moynihan, 2008), and challenges (Ho, 2005) of this process. These studies have employed different methodologies such as case examples (Hoque, 2008), experience-based observations (Sanger, 2008), surveys (Folz, Abdelrazek, & Chung, 2009), and archival secondary data sources (Boyne & Chen, 2006). However, the results are still largely inconclusive. Nonetheless, the breadth and scope of these studies, conceptual papers (Radnor & McGuire, 2003), and review papers (Fryer, Antony, & Ogden, 2009) are impressive. The material is geographically diverse in the European Union (Verbeeten, 2008), the United Kingdom (Kelman & Friedman, 2009), the United States (Ho, 2005; Sanger, 2008), Australia (Hoque & Adams, 2011), and New Zealand (Richardson, 2000) and focuses on many levels of government, including federal, provincial, and municipal (Kuhlmann, 2010). It also covers a broad range of public service delivery functions, not only in different countries but also in different service sectors, including education (Ryan & Feller, 2009), fire service (Kloot, 2009), and health delivery (Kelman, 2006).

Despite a lack of clear substantive evidence of the benefits of PM, public-sector organizations continue to spend significant resources on gathering performance data. In our view, further research is needed to identify processes and practices that can make PM more effective and successful in the public sector (Jaaskelainen & Uusi-Rauva, 2011; Latham, Borgogni, & Pettita, 2008). Of particular interest are the importance of effective implementation of PM (de Lancer Julnes & Holzer, 2001) and the need for research that specifically addresses this issue. For example, what are the common implementation challenges and barriers that government departments and agencies continue to face in implementing PM? What are the key success factors that can result in the more effective implementation of PM in government organizations? How do the context and the characteristics of an organization explain the efficacy of some of these challenges, barriers, and success factors?

This study attempts to address these questions. By employing a qualitative, multi-case study methodology, this research aims to gain a deeper understanding of the factors that affect the implementation of PM in public-sector organizations. The focus of this study is on the federal and provincial levels of government in Canada, as there has been a lack of focus on these two levels of government in previous empirical studies.

In this paper, we use the term *performance management* (*PM*) throughout, as we consider that this term more broadly captures both the improvement and measurement aspects of this approach. The following quote from the Organisation for Economic Cooperation and Development (OECD, 1997) report best describes our position:

> Performance management encompasses performance measurement, but is broader. It is equally concerned with generating management demand for performance information—that is, with its uses in program, policy and budget decision-making processes and with establishing organizational procedures, mechanisms and incentives that actively encourage its use. In an effective performance management system, achieving results and continuous improvement based on performance information is central to the management process. (p. 6)

We begin by providing a review of the relevant background literature on PM in the Canadian public sector.

Background Literature

Since 1995, the Canadian government has required federal departments and agencies to develop strategic objectives and goals as well as plans to measure results and report on them. On an annual basis, departments and agencies are obliged to provide a Report on Plans and Priorities (RPP) with estimates and justification of their spending plans. In addition, they must later provide Departmental Performance Reports (DPRs), which focus on performance measures, both financial and non-financial, as they relate to the commitments made in the RPPs. The Treasury Board of Canada Secretariat (TBS) is the central agency that oversees this process; it provides direction to departments and agencies through policy directives and guidelines (Treasury Board of Canada Secretariat, 2007). This PM process is also practiced at the provincial and municipal levels in those cases where provincial departments and municipalities have to provide annual performance reports. Again, legislation has provided guidelines on the reporting standards for these performance reports (Schatteman, 2010). Therefore, there is a significant amount of PM activity routinely performed in Canadian public-sector organizations. This is no surprise, as the Canadian public sector is not immune to the *New Public Management* focus of governments and the growing concern with accountability and results-based management (Borins, 1995; Kaboolian, 2009).

In Canada, the number of empirical studies on PM in the public sector is limited, with the primary focus on the municipal level of government (Chan, 2004; McDavid & Huse, 2011; Pollanen, 2005). These studies have explored a number of issues, including the type of performance measures being gathered (financial or non-financial), the use of the balanced scorecard, and the perceived usefulness of performance information for decision making (Schatteman, 2010).

The general conclusions of these studies have been that implementing PM systems is seen by both their developers and their users as a useful exercise for the organization. There is also some evidence that PM is being used by politicians to evaluate programs and make decisions related to budgets and funding of programs. However, there is no strong evidence that performance information has been very successful in meeting the goal of improving performance or that it is being used extensively. For example, Chan (2004) studied a specific PM tool, the balanced scorecard, and found that only "about two-thirds of the administrators reported that their organizations have been moderately successful in implementing the balanced scorecard" (p. 216). However, in Chan's (2004) study, administrators also cited a number of factors that can promote successful implementation of PM. These include top management commitment and leadership buy-in, a culture of performance excellence, training and education, clarity of vision, a well-defined strategy, and resources to implement the system.

Another study by Pollanen (2005) examined the use of performance measures in Canadian municipalities and the perceived impediments to their effective use. The findings suggest that senior administrators in Canadian municipalities accept performance measurement, in general, as a useful management tool and work to recognize its potential. However, there was a gap between *desired* use and *actual* use when it came to more challenging measures, such as *effectiveness*, which were more ambiguous and difficult to define.

A study by Schatteman (2010) looked specifically at Ontario municipal governments and their mandated annual performance reports. The author's focus was on the quality of these reports, as perceived by high-ranking local officials such as the chief administrative officer and city manager. The results were not positive: the study found that the quality of the performance reports was generally perceived as low. That is, performance reports were perceived as "not informative, useful or [supportive of] accountability to anyone other than the province of Ontario" (i.e., the funding source) (p. 542).

Schatteman's (2010) results at the municipal level have been reinforced by a study at the provincial level in British Columbia. McDavid and Huse (2011) found in a survey of provincial Members of the Legislative Assembly (MLAs) that the use of performance reports was low. Generally, the reports were seen as a largely symbolic commitment to accountability and the provision of information to high-level legislators. According to McDavid and Huse (2011), "despite their original expectations, the mandated public performance reports have limited utility in improving decision-making related to efficiency and effectiveness, policy-making, or budgeting" (p. 15). In contrast, a recent descriptive study of the City of Lethbridge, by Hildebrand and McDavid (2011), found a greater use of performance reports, because the managers who developed performance measures and the city council members who used the reports shared both a commitment to PM and a view that performance reporting is useful.

The results of the empirical studies in Canada reviewed previously are inconclusive as to the efficacy of PM in Canadian public-sector organizations. Whereas the Hildebrand and McDavid (2011) study had positive results, the other studies found only moderate enthusiasm for PM overall and low usage of or confidence in performance information. All of these studies have focused on the municipal level, with only one focused at the provincial level of government in Canada and none focused at the federal level.

Scope and Purpose of Study

The objective of this study is to examine in more depth how public-sector organizations in Canada are implementing PM. As discussed in the literature review, previous research on public-sector PM in Canada has been mostly at the municipal levels of government. These studies at the municipal level have mostly been quantitative surveys of senior public-sector managers and/or politicians (Pollanen, 2005; Schatteman, 2010) and single case studies or observations of PM practices. The focus has been through the lens of performance measurement experts and/or organizational decision makers (drivers of such practices in the organization), mostly at high levels (McDavid & Huse, 2011). In our view, research on this issue should focus on all levels of the organization, including the employees who have to develop, gather, and report on performance measures related to their work.

In order to achieve this broader perspective, we will focus on the federal and provincial levels of government in this empirical study. We have selected a multi-case qualitative approach. Qualitative research provides an opportunity to examine the organizational context and the deeper issues and meanings that have largely been overlooked in the existing literature on PM. Accordingly, we asked a number of Canadian public-sector organizations at the federal and provincial levels to participate in the study. The benefits of the multi-case study are generally considered limited if fewer than "4 cases are chosen, or more than 10" (Stake, 2006); therefore, we selected five cases to ensure sufficient interactivity between the cases and to ensure data saturation (Creswell, 2007). In-depth interviews were carried out, with a wide spectrum of employees at all levels in each organization, in order to obtain their views and experiences with respect to PM practices. This provided data that are rich in context and also provided a more close-up view of PM, as it is practiced and implemented in Canadian public-sector organizations. From these multi-case studies, we drew insights using a cross-case analysis of the data.

Methodology

Sample

Our sample consisted of five Canadian public-sector organizations, whose characteristics are shown in Table 2.1.

As shown in Table 2.1, four of the case organizations (A, C, D, and E) are at the federal level and one (B) case is at the provincial level. The organizations were selected to reflect a range of sizes and a mix of operational and policy-oriented federal government departments. We also wanted a blend of organizations that were different in structure and mandate such as Crown corporations and special agencies. This purposeful sampling will allow the study to address the research questions proposed earlier, in particular, the impact of

Table 2.1 Sample and Context

ORGANIZATION	A	B	C	D	E
Size	Small: 500 employees	Medium: 1800 employees	Medium–large: 4200 employees	Medium: 2700 employees	Large: 6900 employees
Structure	Headquarters in Ottawa and regional offices	Across the province and includes multiple diverse stakeholders	Headquarters in Ottawa and regional offices	Headquarters in Ottawa and regional offices	Headquarters in Ottawa and regional offices
Sector	Safety and security	Education	Science	Health	Environment
Organization form and jurisdiction	Crown/federal	Department/provincial	Crown/federal	Agency/federal	Department/federal
Data source	8 interviews across 4 branches	12 interviews across 8 divisions	7 interviews in different functional areas	12 interviews with corporate and operational units	8 interviews with corporate and operational units

contextual organizational factors in the implementation of PM within the selected organizations.

We approached our contact person in each organization and obtained the required approvals to carry out the study. At this time, not all of the organizations have agreed to be identified in this paper, so we have provided only some broad contextual information in Table 2.1.

Data Collection and Analysis

We collected data from several sources. First, the key contact in each organization provided important documents on planning and PM in the organization. We reviewed these documents to familiarize ourselves with the organizational context and history of PM. We also reviewed the organizations' websites to gather additional background information on organizational structure, size, and so on. Then, we conducted interviews with key people working at different levels and in different functions across each organization. They included PM program managers (usually residing in a corporate function), other program managers in operational units, and senior functional heads of departments. We used a semi-structured interview protocol for all interviews. The questions focused on strategic planning and PM, performance measurement practices and frameworks, drivers and barriers, integration of PM into the organization's operational activities, and decision making and contributions that PM has made in the organization. The interview schedule was pre-tested with a number of public-sector managers and revised before final use.

Interviews were approximately 1-hour long and were audiotaped and transcribed verbatim. The number of interviews in each organization varied from 7 to 12, as shown in Table 2.1. In total, over a 6-month period, we completed 47 interviews that constituted the data set for the study. Interview data were entered into NVivo 8 to assist in data analysis.

Data were initially analyzed according to the organizing structure of the interview protocol. Within each topic area, emergent themes were identified and summarized. Based on the results of the data analysis, individual case profiles were then prepared for each organization.

Each case profile report was reviewed by all members of the research team and then validated by interview participants to ensure that it accurately captured their perceptions. Once all of the case profiles had been successfully validated, a cross-case analysis was performed. Following Stake (1995, 2006), the four researchers on the study team read each case profile individually and identified any cross-cutting themes or patterns, as well as any discontinuities or contradictions. The team then met in a number of sessions to further refine the analysis by identifying these common themes, patterns, and observations emerging from our individual cross-case analyses. This process is known as *categorical aggregation*, and it involves the researcher seeking a collection of instances from the data and determining issue-relevant meanings that can be placed on them. This is a form of data analysis and interpretation in cross-case analysis suggested by Stake (1995); it also allows the researcher to look for similarities and differences among the cases. The findings and generalizations presented in this paper are based on this cross-case analysis.

Findings

The findings of our cross-case analysis will be presented in three parts. The first part will discuss some of the perceived challenges and barriers that interview participants articulated. Second, a number of success factors are identified from the data, suggesting positive outcomes that these organizations have experienced through implementing PM in their organizations. Third, we will discuss some contextual factors identified in the research.

Challenges and Barriers to Implementing Performance Management

The results of the cross-case analysis demonstrated that the five organizations were at different stages of implementing PM practices. Despite these differences and the varying degrees of success with implementing PM, some common challenges were noted. These challenges fell into five themes: organizational structure and alignment; planning, reporting, and accountability requirements; managing performance data; organizational capacity for PM; and changing mindsets and ownership.

Organizational Structure and Alignment   Alignment was a challenge from several perspectives. First, all of the organizations faced difficulties in achieving and maintaining horizontal alignment—keeping all units of the organization focused on the same overarching organizational goals. There was a tendency for different branches or departments to start functioning in *silos*, with employees focusing inward (within their own organizational unit) and forgetting about how they were contributing to the organization's overall vision and shared goals. To help alleviate this problem, managers in one organization developed a system to track organizational commitments, which they could review regularly across divisions. The system provided an inventory of all the organization's projects, policies, and legislation; commitments to the organization's overall goals; and an update on progress; as such, it provided a forum for ongoing discussion about organizational alignment as well as for operational and strategic planning purposes. To ensure commitment to this initiative, one of the senior executives (assistant deputy minister [ADM]) was assigned responsibility for alignment; he ensured that there was constant attention to *staying the course*, making adjustments, as needed, to achieve re-alignment across the organization.

In all five organizations, PM was housed or *owned* by a corporate services group. Whereas this structure was not inherently problematic, in two of the organizations that had implemented PM less successfully, there was a tendency to view PM as distinctly separate; an attitude of *us* and *them* developed, whereby PM was seen to be *their* responsibility and not something that was shared by the entire organization and that contributed to its overall performance. Defining performance metrics was seen to be something that *they made us do*. It was not integrated into the organization's overall business, and, as a result, it was not aligned across all units.

Vertical alignment was also a challenge. All five organizations experienced difficulties in translating their overall organizational performance goals into achievable, relevant objectives and performance measures at the level of the organizational unit. Cascading these measures down to the level of the individual employee posed an even greater challenge, and a few of the organizations had succeeded in linking individuals' personal performance measures with *corporate* performance goals, thereby driving behavior that supports organizational performance. However, we noted several exceptions. At one organization, for example, senior management had added team-based goals to employees' performance appraisals to reinforce the shift toward a team-oriented matrix structure. At two of the organizations, executive-level pay was clearly linked to achieving specific performance goals.

Planning, Reporting, and Accountability Requirements   One of the mechanisms for promoting organizational alignment is planning—and although the organizations noted that it is critical to link planning to PM, doing so also posed a challenge. At all five organizations, planning and reporting functions were largely defined by relationships with central agencies—specifically, the Treasury Board Secretariat (TBS). However, at three organizations, there was a strong sentiment that TBS planning and reporting mechanisms were significantly constraining. Participants consistently complained that TBS's standardized, hierarchical reporting structures (driven by a strong focus on accountability and transparency) did not reflect the complexity of their organization's business or the horizontal, matrixed nature of many programs. Furthermore, they contended that these planning and reporting mechanisms were inflexible and did not promote learning and improvement. As a result, they faced significant challenges in integrating the TBS-mandated reporting processes with their own ways of doing business and driving performance. In effect, they had to keep *two sets of books* and sometimes separate planning mechanisms.

Managing Performance Data   Effective data management—ensuring data accessibility, integrity, and accuracy—created a challenge for all five organizations. In a number of cases, participants claimed that they had too much data or not necessarily the right data, not in a usable format, and certainly not at their fingertips. In several organizations, PM personnel were using spreadsheets to collect and consolidate performance data from multiple systems across the organization. To address these problems, two of the more successful organizations had made large investments in information systems that would collect and integrate corporate-wide data. For instance, one organization estimated that $100 million was spent on building an information system that harmonized 72 individual systems into one, thus providing a data source from which to extract consistent, reliable data. The second organization had secured funding to integrate several systems through a business intelligence tool set within an Enterprise Resource Planning system. This would allow them to put performance data *on the desktop* of the senior managers/executives in the format of a balanced scorecard. *Most importantly, as one respondent pointed out "many of the data elements that we have in the balanced scorecard to be captured in 'real time', because they're taken from central data sources."*

Related to the data management challenge was the issue of defining metrics—making sure that they were manageable and meaningful. Many of the organizations had too many metrics, had difficultly defining them or agreeing on them, or had difficulty moving away from historical metrics that were *comfortable* or *near and dear to their hearts.* In addition, three of the more science/technology-based organizations expressed frustration at the difficulty of defining operationally oriented metrics in a business where outcomes tend to be achieved over the long term.

There was also the issue of trust and integrity related to data at several organizations. Participants mentioned that there was a need to build trust across organizational units, in order to effectively share data collected by other groups or systems. Questioning the quality or integrity of the data was a tactic employed by some stakeholders to discount decisions taken by management or to dismiss PM in general.

Capacity for Performance Management The capacity for PM varied across the five organizations. In two organizations where PM was less successful, for example, line managers did not appreciate the value that PM could add to the organization and they commonly referred to PM activities as *bothersome, more paperwork,* a *costly overhead expense,* and *time away from real business.* Most saw PM as only an accountability requirement mandated by TBS and not integrally linked to how they do business. In contrast, two other organizations had made concerted efforts to increase their PM capacity through deliberate knowledge-building activities and organizational support, and these efforts had met with significant success.

Low PM capacity in two of the cases stemmed from lack of a clear vision or plan for PM. In the other, more successful organizations, there was a senior executive who was the clear sponsor and champion of PM, who demonstrated clear commitment to and ownership of PM, and who communicated this throughout the organization. This was critical to implementing PM successfully. The challenges in these organizations were *sustaining* the momentum, maintaining a consistent focus through changes in leadership, and ensuring that the PM messages and momentum were not lost. In the provincial organization, for example, interviewees talked about how, despite having several deputy ministers over a period of 7 years, the people on ADM level had managed to *maintains the consistency* and to put their *feet to the fire* to meet metrics and achieve their goals.

Changing Mindsets and Ownership   In the successful organizations, the PM leaders and champions talked about the importance of creating a culture of PM in their organizations. Moving toward a more performance-driven culture means changing mindsets, and several of these organizations had a very strong professional culture, one that would not change readily. Employees were members of particular professions in areas such as science, education, health, and public safety—professions with rigorous training and professional values. In addition, many of the organizations were accustomed to shifting, as required, in reaction to changing political priorities. Performance measurement was considered a *corporate* function and an accountability requirement, something mandated by central agencies to ensure appropriate reporting and control. It was seen as a purely bureaucratic exercise that *takes away* from *real business*—as opposed to a way of *doing* business—and was not seen to be integrated with the overall organizational goals and priorities. Thus, trying to move away from a compliance mentality to one that is more outward-looking and performance-oriented, innovative was a challenge for all.

Success Factors for Effective Performance Management Implementation

As discussed previously, one of the findings of the study was the uneven capacity for PM across the five participating organizations. Overall, whereas two organizations described their PM activities as *in development*, the other three stood out as having achieved a significant level of success with their PM initiatives. By *successful*, we mean that PM was perceived as having a positive effect on the organization and was supported by a significant proportion of employees. Another success indicator was that PM was perceived as being a useful management approach for improving performance and was actively discussed and used for decision making, innovation, and change in the organization. The key success factors noted were a clear vision of PM, integration among PM initiatives, and a strong focus on individual and organizational capacity building.

Clear Vision and Focus   As mentioned previously, all organizations in our study were required to provide performance reports to central agencies. Furthermore, managers in all organizations felt that the reporting frameworks used by these central agencies did not necessarily fit with their own business processes. Nevertheless, managers in the successful organizations were able to develop a vision of using PM to serve the organization apart from central agency requirements.

A key component of this vision was the development of a PM culture. Leaders in these organizations continually talked about the need for a PM culture and reinforced the message by allocating resources to PM initiatives. These organizations also established specific expectations and a clear focus for the distribution of performance information. In all three organizations, a distinct pattern of information delivery was defined, along with a process for using the data, including as a basis for making decisions. For example, one organization collected operational performance information at regional levels that was rolled up to strategic levels for senior managers. High-level *snapshots* were created for some managers, whereas more detailed comprehensive reports were distributed to others. The information flow was defined such that the level of information required was aligned with the role that the manager occupied. As these reports made their way from operational to strategic levels, lessons learned were extracted and considered in light of current operational processes and resourcing strategies.

Finally, leaders in these organizations linked PM to the organization's ability to achieve its overall mission. The use of performance information to focus attention on strategic outcomes, to make mid-course corrections, and to discover areas where processes could be improved formed part of a pervasive message.

Integration of Performance Management Initiatives   An effective practice of the successful organizations was the appointment of a single person or a group responsible for overseeing the development of PM and ensuring its use in the organization. One organization created an integrated team as a structural focal point for PM, including planning, measuring, and reporting. Another organization defined one individual as the PM lead but with accountability shared by all senior managers. The result of having a single coordinating point with shared accountability was better integration among the various PM practices used in the organization. Planning practices, for example, were well linked to the types of performance measures gathered and distributed. In addition, one organization had started an initiative to link business processes to its strategic performance dashboard.

One of the positive outcomes of this level of integration was the building of awareness across the organization that the use of PM practices is the way in which *business is done*. Performance management was not seen as something foreign to the organization; it was integrated into everyday operational activities.

Focus on Capacity Building   Unless people in the organization fully understand PM and how it helps deliver performance outcomes, PM practices are unlikely to be used efficiently. The successful organizations in this study focused on building individual capacity across the organization. To do so, they invested in training and other communication methods to ensure that staff at all levels in the organization truly understood the PM system, its purpose, and its application.

Another related aspect of capacity building was providing the freedom to act on performance information. One of the key characteristics in these organizations was an emphasis on learning from the performance measures rather than using them as an opportunity for *finger pointing*. In one organization, interviewees made the comment that the senior manager was quite interested in *knowing when things were not working, and knowing as quickly as possible,* so that he could help fix the problem. His approach was not to lay blame; it was to resolve the problem before it became a serious issue. Learning from mistakes also helped develop a culture of PM by building trust and reducing employees' fears of speaking openly about performance problems.

In another of the successful organizations, performance problems identified through the analyses of performance measures quickly led to constructive data gathering to address the issue at hand (e.g., distributing research-related information and arranging presentations from experts in the field about how the problem might be resolved). Once again, the message being sent was that the organization was interested in learning about performance problems and would help build knowledge and skills, as needed, to address the problems.

A final element related to capacity building was how to sustain the use of PM practices over time. In other words, how could these organizations build PM capacity into organizational systems, so that PM became *part of the woodwork*? To accomplish this, the successful organizations adapted standard tools such as the balanced scorecard to fit with other PM practices such as budgeting and planning, thus creating a set of mutually reinforcing standard operating procedures. In addition, the implementation of information and communication technologies that enabled rapid delivery of credible performance information enabled the organization to institutionalize PM practices by creating tangible artefacts. The long-term objective was to *stabilize the environment* by building a capacity for PM at the organizational level that could survive political and management changes.

Influence of Contextual Factors

It is instructive to consider the contextual factors that might explain the relative success of these organizations in implementing their PM initiatives. The organizations ranged from small, to medium-sized, to large (500, 1800, and 4200 employees, respectively), but they also operated in different sectors (science, security, and education) and jurisdictions (federal and provincial). In terms of organizational form, at the federal level, both organizations were Crown corporations. However, organization B was a medium-sized, traditionally structured, provincial department. These findings suggest that the initiatives described previously that led to successful implementation of PM are applicable across different types (and sizes) of organizations. However, it is clear that the context in which they operate plays a role. What are these contextual factors? From the cross-case analysis, we have identified three such factors. We believe that these factors have significant explanatory power in explaining how certain organizations can use PM strategically—to inform decision making and drive learning and change.

Organizational Size The first contextual factor that emerged from the cross-case analysis was the size of the organization—both real and *perceived*. Two of the successful organizations (A and B) were physically smaller in size (with fewer employees and less geographic dispersion of organizational units), and this provided several advantages: easier coordination of PM activities, fewer layers of bureaucracy and regional differences to accommodate, and more simplified and centralized communication of a clear vision of PM from senior leadership. Organization A also had the benefit of relative *newness* insofar as it was able to develop a clear mandate for PM and a performance-oriented organizational culture that supported the effort.

However, the third organization managed to be successful in implementing PM, even though it was relatively large in size (C). Despite having 4200 employees, the organizational leadership and employees managed to *think small* in terms of how it operated. In other words, the potential negative effects of size (increased bureaucracy and difficulty in coordination and communication) were mitigated. Like organizations A and B, it was directed by strong leadership who believed in the importance of PM. There was also a clearly articulated vision for PM, and this was communicated throughout the organization.

For larger organizations, the cost of conducting and coordinating capacity-building efforts was higher than that in the smaller organizations. However, organization (C) was creative in capacity building by fostering ongoing communities of PM practice. This more cost-effective mechanism for coordinating the PM effort in a larger organization was implemented throughout the organization. Leadership also recognized the need to invest in these efforts upfront, to ensure that employees were empowered to implement PM, despite the costs.

It can be concluded that although organizational size is a key contextual factor to consider, the challenges of size can be mitigated by ensuring that there is strong leadership, a clear vision for PM, a commitment to capacity building, and a strategy for coordinating efforts across the organization. In other words, large organizations can *think big and act small*.

Complexity of Operating Environment Another important contextual factor was the complexity of the operating environment. The two less successful organizations, organizations D and E, faced very complex operating environments. They had unclear multiple stakeholders, overlapping jurisdictions with other departments, and long-term outcomes that were difficult to measure. This resulted in significant barriers and challenges for them to address. The increased complexity resulted in a proliferation of performance measures that were difficult to comprehend, thereby making the measures less likely to be used for program improvement. The many layers of performance measures also resulted in the need for a complicated *roll-up* exercise across many divisions and departmental units, making it a cumbersome process. Frequently, they lost momentum as a result.

In contrast, organizations A, B, and C had mandates that were clearer and had stakeholders that were more easily identified and *served*. For instance, in the case of organization B (in the education sector), they were parents, teachers, and students, and it had goals that were easier to measure, such as graduation rates and test scores. It also had full funding and control over resources that could be deployed to support the PM initiative. Performance data were easier to manage as a result and were often clearer and more meaningful for users. As a result of the better understanding of the performance measures, these departments could focus their attention on new approaches for improving program outcomes.

Operating Mandate and Form Mandate and the type of organizational form were important contextual factors in the case of the four federal government organizations. The two more successful organizations had clear operational mandates: one was public safety (implementing processes that minimize the risk of public injury) and the other was increased innovation in science through research and patents. As Crown corporations, they also had greater flexibility in budgeting and staffing than regular line departments, allowing for better allocation of resources to meet objectives. This made it easier for them to make decisions to invest in better information systems to capture and provide performance data that were reliable and easily accessible by managers and employees, thus encouraging use.

The less successful organizations had more ambiguous policy mandates (such as improving the health of Canadians and monitoring environmental and pollution impacts) and had to operate under the more restrictive rules of a department. Performance management was seen by these organizations as more paper work and a bureaucratic process, not as something useful. Performance outcome measures were also seen as unrealistic, as they were related to shifting long-term targets that were influenced by many factors beyond the control of the organization. In the case of the environmental agency, overlapping jurisdictions was an important factor, which became a problem when attempting to measure performance.

Discussion and Practical Implications

The findings of this study suggest that public-sector organizations continue to face significant challenges and barriers to implementing PM in their organizations. However, despite these challenges, the findings have also identified some success factors that can improve the effective implementation of PM. Furthermore, an important implication that emerged from this study is the issue of context as an important factor to be considered in understanding PM in the public sector. Previous empirical research and discussions have focused on only finding a universal set of effective PM practices in comparing private- with public-sector organizations. This approach ignores the *within-context* issues in public-sector organizations, which maybe just as important.

These findings are consistent with those of Bititci, Garengo, Dorfler, and Nudurapati (2012), who suggest that the main challenge for PM is to understand the important influence of context. They also argue that this context is changing significantly. A literature review by Jaaskelainen et al. (2012) also point to the need for a contingency approach to PM in the public sector and for identifying patterns among individual case studies. In addition, they argue that contingency factors such as political environment, organization size, and structure should be considered, as we have done in this study. Another paper by Jansen (2004) sets out to develop a contingency framework and approach to measurement and control in govern-mental organizations. Jansen (2004) argues that contingent variables such as ambiguity of organizational objectives, hierarchical position of information users, and the relevance of efficiency and quality can influence the approaches that maybe best to measure performance. This supports the findings of this study related to the complexity of the operating environment and clarity of mandate as important con-textual variables in understanding the implementation success of PM. Empirical work by Jaaskelainen and Sillanpaa (2013) also point to the importance of looking at PM in public organizations by comparing PM practices in different types of public-sector organizations, which we have done in this study.

A summary of the key findings of this study is shown in Table 2.2.

Table 2.2 Summary of Key Findings

CHALLENGES AND BARRIERS TO IMPLEMENTING PERFORMANCE MANAGEMENT

- Alignment: keeping all departments/regions focused on the same performance objectives and goals.
- Translating higher-level performance goals into meaningful operational objectives at lower levels in the organization.
- Dealing with reporting and accountability mechanisms from central agencies that are too rigid, standardized, and constraining; frequently, they do not reflect the realities and complexities of the department.
- Poor performance data management: data not accessible to decision makers in a timely, reliable manner.
- Weak PM capacity and lack of resources, training, and knowledge.
- Loss of momentum: difficulty in sustaining a focus on PM; overtaken by other priorities.
- Lack of ownership of PM, seen as externally driven and just as a bureaucratic exercise and viewed as *their problem* (i.e., the responsibility of just one unit such as corporate services).

SUCCESS FACTORS FOR EFFECTIVE IMPLEMENTATION OF PERFORMANCE MANAGEMENT

- Development of a PM culture with a clear vision of using PM as a strategic management tool (not just an administrative requirement of central agencies).
- Clearly defined PM initiatives, including adequate resource allocation and specific expectations and outcomes.
- Effective data use: PM data used for decision making and operational improvements.
- A dedicated PM team responsible for PM planning, measuring, and reporting responsibilities. This allows for better integration, coordination, and shared accountability of PM initiatives.
- A focus on building capacity for PM (training, communication skills, and understanding of the purpose of PM).

(Continued)

Table 2.2 (*Continued*)   Summary of Key Findings

- An emphasis on learning and not on blame. Problems are identified in order to find solutions and organizational improvements.
- Sustaining PM through integration with other existing performance management tools such as budgeting, planning, balanced scorecard.

INFLUENCE OF CONTEXTUAL FACTORS

- Organizations that were smaller experienced more successful PM implementations and fewer challenges and barriers.
- Larger organizations had to *think small* and required some mitigating practices such as having strong PM leadership and a clear vision and strategy for coordinating PM initiatives across the organization.
- Departments with more complex operating environments (e.g., with ambiguous goals, multiple stakeholders, and overlapping jurisdictions) had more significant barriers to overcome and experienced less success in PM implementation.
- Organizations with less complex operating environments and a single stakeholder found it much easier to identify and develop performance measures that were clearer and more meaningful for users.
- Organizations with clearer mandates found it easier to capture and have reliable performance data available for employee use.
- Having an ambiguous mandate made identifying performance metrics more difficult and resulted in employees having a negative view of PM as more paperwork and a bureaucratic process lacking relevance and usefulness.
- Departments with more independence (e.g., special operating agencies and Crown corporations) found it easier to implement PM initiatives, as they had more flexibility to allocate budget and staffing resources to meet these objectives.

As shown in Table 2.2, we have identified some of the key and continuing challenges and barriers in implementing PM faced by a sample of public-sector organizations in Canada. The study has also identified some of the key success factors that lead to the effective implementation of PM experienced and reported by these organizations. More importantly, our cross-case analysis of the findings identified a number of significant contextual factors that can explain the relative success and different challenges and barriers faced by these public-sector organizations in implementing PM.

Most public-sector organizations cannot escape the requirement to gather performance measures for reporting: it is here to stay. Some practice implications emerging from our findings suggest that a clear linking of PM to strategic activities and outcomes and a message (and actions) from senior management that this is not an add-on activity can be powerful incentives for employees to focus more seriously on PM and to actually *use* the information for improvement. Another implication is that senior managers must develop a performance culture through consistent leadership and a clear message that PM is to be used as an important internal driver of performance improvement and not just as an activity to satisfy external reporting requirements. Therefore, the key strategy is to reposition this activity away from a focus solely on accountability and compliance and more toward the objectives of PM, which are to encourage learning, innovation, and performance improvement. It is also critical to have strong employee buy-in and commitment to PM, so that employees share accountability for and engagement in the development of a PM system (Jaaskelainen & Sillanpaa, 2013).

Conclusions and Future Research

Our study of five Canadian public-sector organizations did not find a consistently strong message that PM is meant to improve performance. Part of the problem is the desire for central agencies to demand performance reports from departments as a routine activity across all departments on a regular annual cycle. This ignores the different role of each department in delivering very different services or in monitoring and ensuring compliance. The required uniformity and enforced templates for performance measurement and reporting are the root causes of the problem. The contextual analysis of this study suggests that governments need to take a more context-sensitive approach when imposing PM frameworks on public-sector organizations. It is critical that they are cognizant that contextual factors such as size and geographic dispersion of public-sector organizations and the complexity of their operating environment can mitigate the success of an imposed rigid one-size-fits-all PM framework. However, this bureaucratic mentality maybe hard to change (Behn, 2003; Radin, 2006).

Our findings suggest that contextual factors can play an important role and have a significant influence on success of PM implementation. Rather than looking for just universal critical success factors, research needs to focus on the impact of context in either enabling or constraining the success of PM implementation in the public sector

(Rhodes et al., 2012). This can result in building a contingency theory of PM implementation such as identifying antecedents and significant contextual factors that can better explain the differences in PM implementation success for public-sector organizations (Boyne, Meier, O'Toole, & Walker, 2006). Clearly, more empirical research is needed to address this knowledge gap. A context perspective can clearly also contribute to future theory building in the field of public-sector PM, having implications for the new public management debate (Borins, 1995; Hood & Peters, 2004; Jaaskelainen & Sillanpaa, 2013).

In conclusion, the findings of this study provide support that public-sector organizations can make PM more effective as a management tool for improving performance. Repositioning PM to focus on it as a useful internal process and developing the needed support mechanisms to make it succeed can result in positive outcomes. However, more importantly, there is a need to take a context-sensitive contingency perspective to PM implementation. Only through this approach can PM become more valued and an effective process for improving the performance of public-sector organizations.

References

Behn, R. (2003). Why measure performance? Different purposes require different measures. *Public Administration Review*, 63(5), 586–606.

Bititci, U., Garengo, P., Dorfler, V., & Nudurapati, S. (2012). Performance measurement: Challenges for tomorrow. *International Journal of Management Reviews*, 14(3), 305–327.

Borins, S. (1995). The new public management is here to stay. *Canadian Public Administration*, 38(1), 122–132.

Boyne, G. A., & Chen, A. A. (2006). Performance targets and public service improvement. *Journal of Public Administration Research and Theory*, 17, 455–477.

Boyne, G. A., Meier, K. J., O'Toole, Jr. L., & Walker, R. M. (2006). Public management and organizational performance: An agenda for research. In G. A. Boyne, K. J. Meier, Jr. L. O'Toole, & R. M. Walker, (Eds.), *Public Service Performance: Perspectives on Measurement and Management*. New York, NY: Cambridge University Press.

Chan, Y.-C. L. (2004). Performance measurement and adoption of balanced scorecards: A survey of municipal governments in the USA and Canada. *The International Journal of Public Sector Management*, 17(3), 204–221.

Creswell, J. W. (2007). *Qualitative inquiry & research design: Choosing among five approaches*. Thousand Oaks, CA: Sage Publications.

de Lancer Julnes, P., & Holzer, M. (2001). Promoting the utilization of performance measures in public organizations: An empirical study of factors affecting adoption and implementation. *Public Administration Review*, 61(6), 693–708.

Folz, D., Abdelrazek, R., & Chung, Y. (2009). The adoption, use and impacts of performance measures in medium-size cities: Progress toward performance management. *Public Performance & Management Review*, 33(1), 63–87.

Fryer, K., Antony, J., & Ogden, S. (2009). Performance management in the public sector. *International Journal of Public Sector Management*, 22(6), 478–498.

Hildebrand, R., & McDavid, J. C. (2011). Joining public accountability and performance management: A case study of Lethbridge, Alberta. *Canadian Public Administration*, 54(1), 41–72.

Ho, A. T. (2005). Accounting for the value of performance measurement from the perspective of Midwestern mayors. *Journal of Public Administration Research and Theory*, 16, 217–237.

Hood, C., & Peters, G. (2004). The middle aging of new public management: Into the age of paradox? *Journal of Public Administration Research and Theory*, 14, 267–282.

Hoque, Z. (2008). Measuring and reporting public sector outputs/outcomes: Exploratory evidence from Australia. *International Journal of Public Sector Management*, 21(5), 468–493.

Hoque, Z., & Adams, C. (2011). The rise and use of balanced scorecard measures in Australian government departments. *Financial Accountability & Management*, 27(3), 308–334.

Jaaskelainen, A., Laihonen, H., Lonnqvist, A., Palvalin, M., Sillanpaa, V., Pekkola, S., & Ukko, J. (2012). A contingency approach to performance measurement in service operations. *Measuring Business Excellence*, 16(1), 43–52.

Jaaskelainen, A., & Sillanpaa, V. (2013). Overcoming challenges in the implementation of performance measurement: Case studies in public welfare services. *International Journal of Public Sector Management*, 26(6), 440–454.

Jaaskelainen, A., & Uusi-Rauva, E. (2011). Bottom-up approach for productivity measurement in large public organizations. *International Journal of Productivity and Performance Management*, 60(3), 252–267.

Jackson, P. M. (2011). Governance by numbers: What have we learned over the past 30 years? *Public Money & Management*, 31(1), 13–25.

Jansen, E. P. (2004). Performance measurement in governmental organizations: A contingent approach to measurement and management control. *Managerial Finance*, 30(8), 54–68.

Kaboolian, L. (2009). Quality comes to the public sector. In R. Cole, & W. R. Scott (Eds.), *The quality movement & organization theory* (pp. 131–154). Thousand Oaks, CA: Sage Publications.

Kelman, S. (2006). Improving service delivery performance in the United Kingdom: Organization theory perspectives on central intervention strategies. *Journal of Comparative Policy Analysis*, 8(4), 393–419.

Kelman, S., & Friedman, J. N. (2009). Performance improvement and performance dysfunction: An empirical examination of distortionary impacts of the emergency room wait-time target in the English National Health Service. *Journal of Public Administration Research and Theory*, 917–946.

Kloot, L. (2009). Performance measurement and accountability in an Australian fire service. *International Journal of Public Sector Management*, 22(2), 128–145.

Kuhlmann, S. (2010). Performance measurement in European local governments: A comparative analysis of reform experiences in great Britain, France, Sweden and Germany. *International Review of Administrative Sciences*, 76(2), 331–345.

Latham, G., Borgogni, L., & Petitta, L. (2008). Goal setting and performance management in the public sector. *International Public Management Journal*, 11(4), 385–403.

McDavid, J. C., & Huse, I. (2011). Legislator uses of public performance reports: Findings from a five-year study. *American Journal of Evaluation*, 32(1), 1–19.

OECD Report. (1997). *In search of results: Performance management practices* (pp. 1–30). Paris: OECD Publications.

Pollanen, R. M. (2005). Performance measurement in municipalities: Empirical evidence in Canadian context. *International Journal of Public Sector Management*, 18(1), 4–24.

Radin, B. (2006). *Challenging the performance movement: Accountability, complexity and democratic values*. Washington, DC: Georgetown University Press.

Radnor, Z., & McGuire, M. (2003). Performance management in the public sector: Fact or fiction? *International Journal of Productivity and Performance Management*, 53(3), 245–260.

Rhodes, M. L., Biondi, L., Gomez, R., Melo, A., Ohemeng, F., Perez-Lopez, G., Rossi, A., & Sutiyono, W. (2012). Current state of public sector performance management in seven selected countries. *International Journal of Productivity and Performance Management*, 61(3), 235–271.

Richardson, R. (2000, October 24–27). *Political accountability and public sector performance management: Exploring the linkages and lessons*. Paper presented at the V International Congress of CLAD on State Public Administration Reform, Santo Domingo, Dominican Republic.

Ryan, K. E., & Feller, I. (2009). Evaluation, accountability and performance measurement in national education systems: Trends, methods, and issues. In K. E. Ryan, & J. B. Cousins (Eds.), *Sage international handbook on educational evaluation* (pp. 171–190). Thousand Oaks, CA: Sage.

Sanger, M. B. (2008). From measurement to management: Breaking through the barriers to state and local performance. *Public Administration Review* (*Special Issue*), S70, 16.

Schatteman, A. (2010). The state of Ontario's municipal performance reports: A critical analysis. Canadian Public Administration, 53(4), 531–550.

Stake, R. (1995). *The art of case study research*. Thousand Oaks, CA: Sage Publications.

Stake, R. (2006). *Multiple case study analysis.* New York, NY: Guildford Press.

Thomas, P. (2007). *Why is performance-based accountability so popular in theory and difficult in practice?* World Summit on Public Governance: Improving the Performance of the Public Sector, Taipei City.

Treasury Board of Canada Secretariat. (2007). *Performance Reporting Good Practices Handbook.* Ottawa: Public Works and Government Services Canada.

Verbeeten, F. (2008). Performance management practices in public sector organizations: Impact on performance. *Accounting, Auditing & Accountability Journal,* 21(3), 427–454.

Wichowsky, A., & Moynihan, D. P. (2008). Measuring how administration shapes citizenship: A policy feedback perspective on performance management. *Public Administration Review,* 68, 908–920. doi:10.1111/j.1540-6210.2008.00931.x.

3

PREPARING FOR ANALYTICS

The Dubai Government Excellence Program

KHALED KHATTAB AND
RAJESH K. TYAGI

Contents

Introduction

Government organizations and the public sector face significant challenges in adopting a result-oriented approach to management and performance. The multiplicity of stakeholders makes it difficult to define a shared vision of *performance excellence*. Regular changes of administration and authorizing environment make it difficult to *maintain constancy of purpose*. Relentless budget shortfalls test the resourcefulness of leaders, managers, budget analysts, and legislators. Nevertheless, with determination and leadership, government organizations have adapted to and adopted proven best practices in performance excellence, derived from international private- and public-sector organizations, as well as international business excellence frameworks such as the European Foundation for Quality Management (EFQM: www.efqm.org), to change the culture from one focused on compliance to the one focused firmly on results and customer centricity (Ahrens, 2013, 2014).

The United Arab Emirates (UAE) is a federation consisting of seven emirates located on the Arabian Gulf, and its capital is Abu Dhabi. Dubai is the second largest of the seven emirates. It is the most populous city and often makes headlines because of its significant investment in grandiose real estate projects, its commitment to continuous development of the financial sector, and its tourism and hospitality industry. In the span of 45 years, Dubai has transformed itself from a traditional pearl-diving village-based economy to a modern knowledge-based economy. It was a small fishing port, and despite the fact that less than 95% of its gross domestic product (GDP) is not oil-based, it is now one of the fastest growing cities in the world, attracting people from all over the globe to live a life of comfort, economical gains, and an unprecedented level of social security. It is expected that by 2020, oil will account for less than 1% of Dubai's GDP and tourism will produce more than 20% of the GDP (Dubai Statistical Year Book, 2013). Currently, nonmanufacturing industry makes the largest contribution (48%) to the UAE's GDP, followed by services (38%), manufacturing (12%), and agriculture (2%) sectors (Global Competitiveness Report, 2013–2014). The country's economic development has been possible largely due to its emphasis on building macroeconomic strength, political stability, reliable institutions, state-of-the-art infrastructure, and knowledge-intensive clusters.

HH Sheikh Mohammed bin Rashid Al Maktoum is UAE's Vice-President, Prime Minister, and Ruler of Dubai. He is the visionary and driving force for the improvement of government organizations' performance in Dubai and the UAE through different institutional programs and awards focused primarily on advancing performance, sustainable management systems, continual improvement, and human and leadership development, as well as through instilling a culture of excellence in Dubai and the UAE. Under his leadership, Dubai has undertaken major reforms in the UAE's government, starting with the UAE Federal Government Strategy in 2007. Dubai has launched UAE Vision 2021 with the aim of making the UAE *one of the best countries in the world* by 2021.

The objective of this chapter is to provide an overview of the Dubai Government Excellence Program (DGEP) and Model and to describe the evolution of the performance management system in the Dubai Government and its strategy for sustaining a culture of excellence. The chapter is divided into four sections. The first section introduces the DGEP and Model. The second section describes the evolution of the performance management system in Dubai and the Dubai strategic plan. The third section discusses the impact of the DGEP on performance. The final section discusses the opportunity for sustaining the culture of excellence in Dubai.

This chapter is based on the analysis of 30 organizations that received the DGEP award in Dubai. These organizations have continuously used the DGEP's excellence criteria for government organizations as a management framework and as one of several tools for continuous improvement purposes and have demonstrated a high level of consistent improvement in their performance and stakeholders' satisfaction. The authors have reviewed and examined reports, award submissions, and internal documents on organizational excellence and quality and have used information available in the public domain. The names of the organizations are kept confidential for obvious reasons, and an aggregate analysis is provided in this chapter. This chapter emphasizes the following points in particular:

- The adoption of organizational excellence frameworks can help improve performance of government organizations.
- Leadership is critical to drive performance in government organizations.
- Continuous learning and development are key elements in sustaining the culture of excellence.

Dubai Government Excellence Program

Since 1997, the DGEP has honored numerous government organizations in Dubai for outstanding achievements. Administered by the General Secretariat of the Executive Council of Dubai, DGEP presents awards to government organizations in Dubai that have displayed outstanding performance. This coveted award is tangible evidence of an organization's level of excellence. Government organizations in Dubai are mandated to participate in the DGEP assessments, which is the driving force behind the continual performance improvement among those organizations since the program's inception. High-performance organizations see excellence as a way to boost customer satisfaction, employee productivity, profitability, and stakeholders' value, while cutting costs and reducing waste. Organizations that demonstrate excellence follow a steady, incremental path over several years and also tend to invest heavily in people, programs, and processes that continuously improve their environment, using a roadmap to performance excellence (Hutton, 1994).

Ideal goal of DGEP is to enable government organizations to achieve welfare and happiness for citizens and residents in Dubai. It also aspires to meet the community's needs and expectations to reach the highest degree of efficiency and effectiveness in the provision of government services. Furthermore, it aims to support government trends related to innovation to acquire a competitive advantage and a leading position. It constitutes a roadmap for governments that seek to transform themselves into leading, innovative, and smart government. The approach serves as an example of the best government practices through developing a set of principles, including effectiveness, efficiency, learning, and development, and the use of modern concepts, such as those related to innovation, future shaping, and integration as part of the government work.

Dubai Government Excellence Program aims at spreading the concept of excellence, innovation, quality, best management, and professional practices in the government sector in Dubai. It is also mandated to develop excellence models, assess government organizations, and select award winners. Its vision is to attain international levels of excellence in government performance in Dubai, and in 2007, the program received the United Nations Public Service Award for improving the delivery of services in government organizations.

The DGEP Model is built around the European Foundation for Quality Management (EFQM) Model, with an extra emphasis on innovation and transparency. Many business excellence models, especially the EFQM Model, have evolved from a means of recognizing and promoting excellence service, based on the eight excellence dimensions and on total quality management; for example, it determines the theoretical platform for world-class performance. Dubai Government Excellence Program is a unique business excellence model that allocates substantial resources toward improvement of the participating organizations' process based on the best-practice excellence models. The criteria for assessing and rewarding distinguished projects includes customer satisfaction and employees satisfaction sometimes evaluated through mystery shoppers' surveys. This program is recognized by many as the foundation for organizational improvement because it promotes a degree of competition not normally seen in public sector organizations. In addition, the pre-defined criteria provides specific targets that encourages senior officials, managers and employees to continuously improve program outcomes.

External assessors carry out EFQM assessments. Consulting firms conduct the measurements of customer satisfaction and employee satisfaction. They also provide mystery shoppers to compare actual services with their various process targets (helpfulness, speed, completeness, and so on). External trainers run general quality and excellence trainings for government employees and specialized workshops to train internal EFQM assessors (250 individuals certified in 2011). A multi-agency team made up of members of different government entities promotes knowledge transfer between government entities.

There are more than 65,000 employees working in these government organizations in Dubai, which serve not only the entire population of Dubai, which is in the order of 1.8–2.0 million, but also the visitors of Dubai (tourists, investors, and so on), which numbered 18 million in 2008. A key element of the work of the DGEP is the Government Excellence Award. It is awarded for 19 categories that are divided into two groups: institutional excellence and employee excellence. Underlying these awards is the standard EFQM model with enablers and results. Dubai Government Excellence Program not only awards the winners in each category, but it also seeks to further motivate each participating entity through a report that explains its strengths and areas for improvement based on the excellence model evaluation.

Dubai Government Excellence Program's Excellence Model
and Evolution of Performance Management in Dubai Government

The Dubai Government launched DGEP to overcome the following shortfalls/inefficiencies in the government departments:

- Managers are performing tasks that could be done easily by their subordinates.
- Overlapping of roles and responsibilities among managers/functions.
- Waiting for information, which leads to delays in performing work and making decisions.
- Spending more than the necessary.
- Complex decision-making process (e.g., even for a simple low-value procurement of goods, one can find too many committees holding up/delaying decision making).
- Lack of appreciation of the management system.
- Lack of authority/empowerment of employees.
- Inefficient processes—bureaucratic processes with built-in non-value-adding tasks.
- Ineffective processes—processes without any clear focus/end result.
- Complex/fragmented business processes, and lack of process ownership, involving too much inter-department coordination.
- Lack of standardization of work.
- Excessive dependence on post-delivery audits rather than risk identification and mitigation.

The Government Sector in Dubai has come a long way in the last years. A brief calendar of the progress is as follows:

- In early 2000 after the introduction of DGEP, government organizations were required to develop strategic plans and performance measures as part of their budget requests.
- Best practices were brought from the private sector to support management improvement in the government. Consultants from different companies were brought in to develop a management model and to train managers and internal performance consultants on the principles of strategic planning and performance measurement.

- Total quality management, continuous quality improvement, and service quality initiatives emerged in government organizations, and some of them began training staff in continuous process improvement methods.
- Government organizations were required to adopt a management model based on the principles outlined above and to appoint an internal advisor to lead the effort.
- The Executive Council provided technical assistance to government organizations in developing performance management systems and strategic plans.

Figure 3.1 provides an overview of the DGEP Framework based on the EFQM.

As a result of the implementation, significant progress has been made in changing the culture and in improving performance. On the ground, service delivery has improved in timeliness, accuracy, and responsiveness. Customers can access all government services online 24/7 from the comfort of their own home or office. Revenue-generating organizations actively benchmark their processes and production against private-sector counterparts and show up favorably in those comparisons. Managers have access to better operational data.

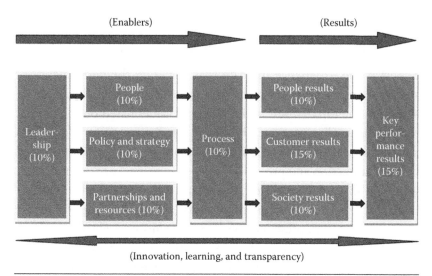

Figure 3.1 Dubai Government excellence program framework.

Considerations in Bringing *Performance Excellence* to the Government Sector

The execution was backed up by a decree signed by the Ruler of Dubai, mandating the participation of all government departments in DGEP, where they are assessed annually by independent and external assessors who do not reside in Dubai, in order to ensure transparency. In other words, all government departments were forced to participate in the annual assessments through a top-down authoritative approach.

Results of the first cycle of assessments were shocking, and the scores were poor. The Ruler warned the top management of all government departments, especially the low-scoring ones, that they would all be fired. He gave them 2 years to improve their performance. Some of the EFQM criteria were adapted and others were added in order to suit the overall business environment in Dubai and the local culture of the UAE, such as:

- People management.
- The environment.
- Emiratization (increasing the number of local UAE citizens in all government departments, especially in the jobs suffering from low numbers of locals).
- Specialized leadership development programs for local people.
- The development of a second/backup leadership team in all organizations.
- The reinforcement of quality, health, safety, and environment standards and management systems.

Research and experience indicate that changing the performance of any large organization starts with clear, sustained, disciplined leadership from the top that sets a direction and values based on the desired results. Those directives are translated into better performance in a sustainable way only if the activities of managers and staff are aligned with that direction and progress is tracked in a regular and data-driven way from the top. In addition, the reward structures of the organization must reinforce the desired behaviors and results. Just as in other sectors, this section presents a few key elements critical to the success of performance management system in the government sector: clear and consistent leadership from the top, engagement of citizens, and alignment of strategies with priorities.

Clear and Consistent Leadership from the Top

Because the leader appoints directors directly, and they serve *at the pleasure* of the leader, those directors are often highly responsive to the leader's directives. A leader who exercises his authority to establish expectations for performance can have significant impact. The directors should be asked to develop performance contracts with the leader and to report progress quarterly. Many directors cascaded the concept into their departments, requiring performance contracts and regular reports from their direct reports. Those directors reported that the *performance contract* model helped them align staff efforts around the priorities identified in the contract with the public organization's leader.

This leader should also sharpen the focus on management accountability by requiring all directors to personally and visibly review operational performance data. In addition, the leader and his directors should exemplify the principles of performance leadership by the following:

- Articulating the results to be achieved, as well as the guiding values and behaviors.
- Allocating resources and providing sponsorship in support of the desired results.
- Relentlessly and visibly reviewing performance against targets.
- Supporting the development of a culture in which innovation and learning can happen.
- Engaging stakeholders in evaluating the results achieved.

Engagement of Citizens in Defining Desired Results and Assessing Performance

The private sector aims to *delight* its customers, whereas applying the same strategies in the public sector is challenging. Rangers in public parks might have voluntary customers, whereas the police officers on the highways must define *customer service* differently. Instituting a *customer focus* in regulatory organizations has been challenging; their *customers* are not always *right*. In addition, public organizations distinguish between two sets of *customers*: the direct recipients of their services are *customers* in that they receive the output of their work. The general public and those who benefit from government are also considered by many government employees to be *customers*, and they often have radically different expectations from those of the service recipients.

Government organizations should be charged with being citizen-centered and customer-oriented. This means that regulatory organizations must define *customer service* differently than business does; *customer service* in regulatory organizations is not about *delighting customers* but rather about conducting regulatory functions authorized in the general public interest in a way that does not create an undue administrative burden on the *customers* of the public organizations. On an even higher level, we need to be looking at how we engage citizens as citizens in the work of government. Citizens are more than *consumers* of government products, and they are interested in more than a *return on their investment*. They also expect *equity* and a variety of *protections*. It is not enough to be *doing things right*; organizations must also be working with citizens to determine if they are *doing the right things*.

Alignment of Strategies with Priorities

Government organizations in Dubai are required to submit strategic plans and performance measures with their budget submittals. This requirement was a paradigm shift for all organizations.

As a result, the definition of *performance* became clearer: staff, managers, and legislators could have more meaningful dialogues about the linkage between resources and results and the value added at each link in the chain. Process improvement efforts could be prioritized on the basis of their potential for contributing to those results, and cross-organizational efforts were emerging naturally from the shared vision.

For the first time, government organizations could see that strategic plans and measures can be valuable allies in making a case for funding, and the demand for training in performance measures, excellence, and quality has grown dramatically!

Dubai Strategic Plan 2015 and Dubai Plan 2021

In 2007, the Government of Dubai laid out Dubai Strategic Plan (DSP) 2015 and then the Dubai Plan 2021 in 2015. Both plans were heavily dependent on information gathered since 1997 through DGEP assessments. The government's ambitions were best summarized by

DSP 2015. Through DSP 2015, Dubai established its first documented long-term strategy, making it one of the first to do so in the region. Dubai Strategic Plan 2015 outlined the Dubai's strategic priorities in five main areas: economic development; social development; security, justice, and safety; infrastructure, land, and environment; and government excellence.

Dubai Strategic Plan 2015 set ambitious targets for Dubai's growth for the long-term, highlighting key sectors of focus and priorities areas that would shape the emirate as it continued its march forward. Dubai Strategic Plan 2015 was the driver for change in many sectors and was the basis for the development of the Government of Dubai's sector strategies and several other reform initiatives. However, above all, DSP 2015 offered guidance to government entities and other players crucial to the Dubai story that helped ensure coordination among the various stakeholders in pursuit of the vision of the leadership. Dubai has had considerable achievements over the last several years, putting the emirate on the fast track of development. Figure 3.2 outlines the key objectives in the DSP.

Dubai Plan 2021 addresses the urban environment, including both natural and built assets, and looks at the living experience of the people of Dubai and its visitors as a result of their interaction with this environment and the economic and social services provided. In addition, the plan also focuses on the economy, which is the city's development engine, and its fuel for its march forward. One of the six themes, *A pioneering and Excellent Government*, focuses on such a topic.

Figure 3.2   Key objectives in the Dubai strategic plan.

Impact of Dubai Government Excellence Program
on the Government's Performance

Dubai Government Excellence Program developed its excellence criteria with assistance from professionals from across the public service and EFQM network (Dubai Government Excellence Program, 2015). Dubai Government Excellence Program is founded on the excellence principles, and it also serves as the basis for adjudication of the DGEP Awards, under the banner of the *DGEP Awards for Excellence*; the awards are Dubai's own awards for recognizing outstanding achievement.

Some results reported by DGEP are as follows:

- Improvement in employee turnover.
- Increase in cost savings.
- Increase in customer satisfaction over an average of a 4-year period.
- Increase in employee satisfaction.
- Reduction in cycle time.

Discussion and Conclusion

Government organizations in Dubai have adapted the DGEP excellence criteria and have been explicitly using the criteria as the foundation for regular organization self-assessments, engaging staff across each organization in identifying opportunities to improve. Most importantly, the organizations act on the identified opportunities and prioritize projects to address them. Based on the analysis, we can identify key characteristics of organizations that have received the DGEP Award:

- *Visible and committed leadership*: Personal involvement of executives is required to drive performance in any organization. The public organization's leader is a key link between the organization and its stakeholders.
- Demonstrated positive impact of cross-functional business processes.
- Higher level of employee commitment and engagement.
- Comprehensive performance measurements.
- A culture of excellence.

Government organizations' managers can benefit from the application of best practices and management models from the private sector. However, the effective application in the public sector of a management principle developed in the private sector is not straightforward. Significant translation of terminology and modification of the approach maybe necessary. For instance, in the regulatory organizations, employees are highly resistant to the concept of *customer service*. Their *customers* are not *always right*, and until we are able to clarify the customer requirements that regulatory organizations should be expected to meet, the customer-based vocabulary of *quality* would impede acceptance of other valid principles of continuous quality improvement. In the government sector, alternatives for recognizing performance do not include stock options, yearly bonuses, or other perks available in large private corporations. In government, one of the most meaningful rewards of good management is a bigger budget (or, these days, a smaller cut). Managerial interest in measuring and using performance will markedly become more evident if a budget-building process is introduced and informed by measures of effectiveness. If the performance management process is aligned with the budget, this will create the motivation for managers to take a more thoughtful approach to the selection and use of measures in their programs.

In a multi-level case study using in-depth interviews and questionnaires, implementation issues with DGEP were studied (McAdam et al., 2013). The research found considerable variation in the implementation effectiveness across the different levels within the organization. Overall, there was an acceptance of the business improvement side of the total quality management aspects.

The Government of Dubai is committed to improving the customer experience among all of the government departments and to sustain the culture of excellence in the long term. They have established and executed a clear and comprehensive customer-centricity strategy based on the following:

- *Identification of different customer groups/segments*: Government of Dubai identified different customer groups per the government departments serving them.
- *Development of new and improved services*: Based on the needs and expectations of different customer groups, the

government developed new and/or improved public services, and all departments were mandated to introduce e-services and then mobile/smart services. Today, all services can be requested through smart phones.

- *Listening to customers continually*: Customer satisfaction surveys, customer complaints, and mystery shopping are some of the most commonly used structured channels for listening to the voice of the customer.

- *Establishing service quality index*: Similar to financial or operational performance index/metrics, the government developed a service quality index based on the outcomes/measures resulting from customer-listening methods. This is called the *Dubai Service Model*, which was developed and implemented at each department level, and it also got aggregated at the entire government level.

- *Service standards*: The government established customer experience standards/codes that shaped and supported every aspect of the customer experience. Standards were developed with a focus on reliability, responsiveness, assurance, empathy of service design, and delivery, including tangibles.

- *Outreach/education*: The government reached out to various customer groups/segments to support service awareness and educate service users on how to derive maximum value from services. The focus was on convenience to customer, reliability, availability of services, and ease of doing business with the government.

- *Service recovery*: They established a process of responding to service delivery that did not meet or exceed the customer's original expectations.

- *Establishing comprehensive measurement and review system*: In order to achieve the vision, mission, and strategic goals, they established a qualitative and quantitative measurement framework covering performance of all the stakeholders (i.e., customers, employees, partners, society, and regulators).

- *Strategic measures linked to the vision*: They ensured that measures were linked to vision and mission, so that achievement/ progress toward fulfillment of vision and mission could be measured and monitored.

- *Development of lagging and leading indicators*: Where feasible, they established lagging indicators based on leading indicators, such as customer satisfaction with on-time delivery of services (lagging indicator) and the time taken to deliver a service (leading indicator).
- *Establishing measures of effectiveness and efficiency*: They included measures of effectiveness and efficiency, such as customer satisfaction with the quality of resolution of complaint (measure of effectiveness) and the time taken to resolve complaint (measure of efficiency).

References

Ahrens, T. (2014). Tracing the evolution of the Dubai Government Excellence Program. *Journal of Economic and Administrative Sciences*, 30(1), 2–12. Accessed January 2015.

Ahrens, T. (2013). Assembling the Dubai Government Excellence Program - A motivational approach to improving public service governance in a monarchical context. *International Journal of Public Sector Management*, 26(7), 9–19.

Dubai Government Excellence Program (DGEP). (2015). Excellence criteria and award categories. https://www.egec.gov.ae/en/council-members/dubai-government-excellence. Accessed January 2015.

Hutton, D. W. (1994). *The change agents' handbook: A survival guide for quality improvement champions*. Milwaukee, WIL: ASQ Quality Press.

McAdam, R., W. Keogh, A. Adhmed el Tigani, and P. Gardiner. (2013). An exploratory study of business excellence implementation in the United Arab Emirates (UAE) public sector: Management and employee perceptions, *International Journal of Quality & Reliability Management*, 30(4), 426–445.

Schawb, K. (Ed.). (2013). Global competitiveness report, 2013–2014. World Economic Forum. https://www.weforum.org/reports/global-competitiveness-report-2013-2014.

PART III

APPLICATIONS AND CASE STUDIES

4

Leveraging Innovation Systems

Supporting Science and Technology Capability Analysis through Big *Messy* Data Visualization

ANDREW VALLERAND, ANTHONY J. MASYS, AND GARY GELING

Contents

Introduction

Canada must prepare for a future characterized by dynamic and uncertain threat and risk landscape. Ensuring the safety and security of Canadians calls for not only supporting defense initiatives but also contributing to more secure borders, enhancing the resiliency of cyber and other critical infrastructure, and responding to natural disasters, humanitarian crises, and health emergencies. Science and technology

(S&T) is essential for ensuring the defense of Canada and represents a critical element of national security. As such, the S&T and the broader innovation system are indispensable capabilities that contribute to operational excellence and effective, evidence-based decision making.

The Department of National Defence (DND), the Canadian Armed Forces (CAF), and their safety and security partners depend on S&T to deliver on their respective mandates and adapt to ever-changing demands. Defence Research and Development Canada (DRDC) is the primary delivery agent for the departmental S&T investment. It operates at the center of an innovation community whose members provide ideas, technology, and knowledge. The key challenge before this community is to integrate these efforts in a way that effectively leverages capacity, draws on the strengths of all who collaborate, and is best suited to the client's requirements. Collaboration with key S&T partners is pursued in a strategic fashion, focusing on areas of greatest impact and alignment with departmental and government priorities. Recognizing this requirement, DRDC sponsored a *pilot project* to examine *S&T Situational Awareness* (Vallerand et al., 2016) in the health sciences sector within the S&T Capability Communities of Practice (CoPs). To perform this analysis, we have combined a recently published and contextualized Zachman Architecture Framework (Zachman, 2003) with a well-documented Social Network Analysis (SNA) (Masys, 2014) to visualize *360° views* of each S&T Capability. Such novel views generate not only a wealth of insights but also unique situational awareness related to what may correspond to the *pulse* or *health* of any S&T Capability CoPs (internal and external).

Big *Messy* Data

In today's data-rich environments, "...*governments have unprecedented opportunities to tap into their own data-rich sources of intelligence to improve performance and reduce costs...Utilizing available data can equip government leaders with a powerful tool for gathering valuable intelligence to inform planning and decision making*" (CGE, 2015). Through the advent of Big Data analytics patterns, correlations and trends can be revealed to yield deep insights that support successful change. Within the defense and security domain, through S&T initiatives and innovation partnerships, data are generated at an unprecedented scale from a wide range of sources. Therefore, the way we view and manipulate the big *messy* data requires new approaches in order to discover new insights from unstructured data sources. Visualization of large volumes of data facilitates data exploration, thereby helping to identify valuable data patterns and anomalies. Within government, Big Data analytics enhances the organization's capability to make evidence-based decisions by providing greater visibility and transparency of the organization's impact profile by uncovering the hidden value of messy data within the defense, security, and safety domains.

Network Analysis

Social Network Analysis facilitates understanding of a group of *actors* through a structured analysis that leverages the domains of mathematics, anthropology, psychology, and sociology. The methodology and visual thinking approach focus on uncovering the patterning of people's interaction and interpreting the network attributes to facilitate better understanding regarding the behavior of the network. Social Network Analysis is a key methodology that supports defense and security applications (Masys, 2014). From counter-terrorism to organizational analysis and design, SNA supports the determination of key actors of any social network, so as to understand their importance or influence in a network. The networks can be modeled as a generalized network (graph) consisting of nodes and links (Figure 4.1).

Social Network Analysis methods help identify groups of actors that are more *densely connected* among each other than with the rest of the network, thereby providing insights regarding collaboration,

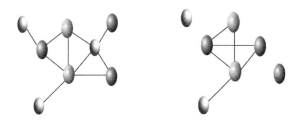

Figure 4.1 Social network examples (nodes and links) of a densely or more loosely connected network.

information sharing, and flow. To a large extent, SNA relies on a mathematical model in the form of a graph and a set of algorithms that traverses the graph in various ways to analyze the network. Centrality reveals how important, influential, or powerful a node is, which may reflect the roles of actors in a network. The SNA approach is well documented in Masys (2014, 2016) and Gunduz-Oguducu and Etaner-Uyar (2014).

Zachman Framework

In today's complex defense, security, and safety environments, many organizations have great difficulty responding to change. Part of this difficulty is due to opaqueness in collaborative networks and the complex value chain that shapes investments and strategic decision making. The Zachman Framework provides a means of classifying an organization's architecture. It is a proactive business tool, which can be used to model an organization's existing functions, elements, and processes.

The Zachman Enterprise Architecture Framework is a classification scheme represented visually as a table or a matrix with columns and rows. Each cell within the matrix provides a unique model or representation of the enterprise. The information in each row of the matrix would be relevant to the particular person in the enterprise viewing it (Zachman, 2003). Overall, the Zachman Enterprise Framework can be viewed as a tool for creating knowledge, clarifying thinking, and as an aid in analysis and decision making.

Matrix Columns

The columns represent the *interrogatives* or questions that are asked of the enterprise.

These are as follows:

- *What* (data): What are the business data, information, or objects?
- *How* (function): How does the business work; that is, what are the processes in business?
- *Where* (network): Where are the business's operations?

- *Who* (people): Who are the people that run the business, what are the business units, and what is their hierarchy?
- *When* (time): When are the business processes performed; that is, what are the business schedules and workflows?
- *Why* (motivation): Why are the processes, people, or locations important to the business; that is, what are the business drivers or business objectives?

The framework enables complex subjects to be distilled into systematic categories, using these six basic questions. The answers to these questions will differ, depending on the perspective or audience (represented in the rows).

Matrix Rows

Each row represents a distinct view of the organization, from the perspective of different audiences. These are ordered in a desired priority sequence.

Zachman Framework: Contextualized for Defence Research and Development Canada

Cross and Parker (2004, p. 13) argue that "*…in today's flatter organizations, work of significance demands effective collaboration within and across functional, physical and hierarchical boundaries.*" Making successful and impactful strategic investments depends on an organization's ability to understand its networks and collaborative relationships. Research shows that appropriate connectivity in well-managed networks within organizations can have a substantial impact on performance, learning, and innovation (Cross and Parker, 2004, p. vii).

Given the dynamic threat and risk landscape that defines the safety and security domain, what is needed is a more targeted approach to improving collaboration and network connectivity. It is well documented that "*…managers who target strategic points in social networks can quickly increase an organization's effectiveness, efficiency and opportunities for innovation*" (Cross and Parker, 2004, p. 8), including the ability to innovate differently (i.e., faster and bigger). Understanding the collaborative space is a key requirement for achieving these outcomes. The S&T Capability domain associated with the defense, security, and safety landscape is a distributed network of people, processes, and technologies. The result of such a capability fundamentally emerges as a *knowledge artifact*. The collaborative space described leverages diverse perspectives, knowledge, and experiences in shaping the analysis of the future security landscape, thereby contributing to the capability planning, management, and integration. Understanding the impact of S&T investments within the defense, security, and safety domains derived from the analysis requires interrogation of the *messy* data to visualize the S&T landscape. It is through this *visualization* that *communities of practice* emerge that can be leveraged to support greater impact of the S&T investment. Similarly, key outliers can be identified and connected to the *community of practice* to support enhanced collaboration.

The Zachman Architecture Framework (Zachman, 2003) is one method of conceptualizing and visualizing a comprehensive picture (*360° view*) of an organization. In so doing, the Zachman Framework supports the messy data analysis as a model or classification schema that organizes descriptive representations. Contextualized for DRDC, it provides a holistic view of the expected impact of an S&T Capability, thereby identifying successes, gaps, shortcomings, and opportunities to impact or influence stakeholders needing the S&T within the defense, security, and safety domains. The Zachman Framework is a validated six-by-six classification schema, where the six rows represent different perspectives (or *levels*) of the enterprise (i.e., an S&T Capability) and the six columns illustrate different aspects rooted in the foundational questions: *Who*, *What*, *Where*, *When*, *How*, and *Why* in the actual S&T Capability (Figure 4.2). To ensure a complete and

Figure 4.2   Foundational questions of Zachman Framework. (Adapted from Zachman, J.A., The Zachman framework: A primer for enterprise engineering and manufacturing, 2003, http://www.zachmaninternational.com, accessed February 8, 2016.)

holistic understanding of the enterprise architecture, it is necessary to develop an approach that address the six *perspectives* and six *interrogatives* that constitute the rows and columns, respectively, of the framework.

Not only are the above-mentioned six questions particularly important for building the CoP in and around the S&T Capability, but also knowing the *level* of the *What*, the actual data *level*, is crucial. Whether the data are supporting at the strategic level, at the operational level, or at the tactical level is of paramount importance for three reasons. *First*, such unique (contextualized) levels help visualize the level at which S&T performers are actually performing their work. *Second*, it helps set plans and targets to consider altering the trajectory of a particular team; for instance, the work may remain at the tactical level and may never be elevated to the strategic level to the benefit of senior clients/leaders in the agency that actually invests in the (people, laboratory equipment, and infrastructure that make up the internal) S&T Capability. *Third*, this visualization helps treat the S&T CoP as a *Functioning Enterprise*. The above-mentioned three points thus enable the emergence of an enterprise strategy. They also enable a transformative management approach to the knowledge spawned by that internal/external S&T Capability. In this way, a Zachman Architecture Framework is used to visualize the mapping of outputs to the level of expected impact holistically in an S&T Capability, a highly desirable attribute. By design, it can provide the data needed to alter plans and set targets for different levels of impact, from the S&T Capability.

Visualization of the Innovation Space: Network Analysis

Understanding collaboration networks, the focus on relations, and the patterns of relations requires a set of methods and analytic concepts that are distinct from the methods of traditional statistics and data analysis (Wasserman and Faust, 1994, p. 3). The visual representation of data that a graph or sociogram offers facilitates an analysis of the connectivity and patterns that might otherwise go undetected (Wasserman and Faust, 1994, p. 94).

Common SNA applications that resonate with the S&T innovation domain include the following:

- Supporting partnerships and alliances.
  - Cross-organizational initiatives leverage organizations' unique capabilities. Social Network Analysis can illuminate the effectiveness of such initiatives in terms of information flows, knowledge transfer, and decision making.
- Assessing strategy execution.
  - Core competencies or capabilities in knowledge-intensive work are usually a product of collaboration across functional or divisional boundaries. Social Network Analysis determines whether the appropriate cross-functional or departmental collaborations are occurring to support strategic objectives.
- Improving strategic decision making.
  - Mapping information flows and decision points.
- Integrating networks across core processes.
  - Social Network Analysis provides a diagnostic assessment of information and knowledge flow, both within and across functions critical to a core process.
- Promoting innovation.
  - Innovation is a collaborative endeavor. One needs to assess how a team is integrating its expertise and the effectiveness with which it is drawing on the expertise of others within the organization. In addition, assessment of the degree of interdisciplinary S&T present to potentially innovate differently is important.
- Ensuring integration post-merger or large-scale change.
  - Social Network Analysis assessments reveal significant issues that leaders need to address for the initiatives to be successful.
- Developing CoPs.
  - Uncovering key members of the community and assessing overall health in terms of connectivity (Cross and Parker, 2004, pp. 8–9).

The dynamic threat and security environment requires an S&T posture that is agile and adaptable. The S&T innovation posture should adapt when new projects demand different kinds of information and expertise. Ideally, the innovation networks can surge: sense opportunities or problems and rapidly tap into the right expertise for an effective response. As new challenges and opportunities arise, S&T CoPs need to identify relevant expertise—who knows what in the network (Cross and Parker, 2004, p. 31).

Methodology

To examine the S&T impact and collaborative networks within DRDC, we examined the health sciences sector within the S&T Capability domain. We used the keywords in the titles of each S&T Capability* in health sciences and their documented sub-domains (Comeau et al., 2015) to search the unclassified Canadian published literature (CANDID, MEDLINE, WEBofSCIENCE, Canada, all Provinces) and the five-eyes published literature (AUS DSTO, UK DSTL, USA DTIC, DRDC Virtual Library, MEDLINE, NTIS, SciTech CONNECT, WEBofSCI, all 5 TTCP Nations individually, including NATO literature [NATO STO]). From the 6 complete years of 2010–2015, about 900 reports were located, but only 752 reports that directly related to the topics at hand were kept for the analysis. Based on the recently published Zachman Architecture

---

* 4.1: Personal CBR Protection S&T Capability; 4.2: Blast Protection Injury S&T Capability; 4.4: Military Medicine S&T Capability; and 4.5: Medical Countermeasures (MCM) to CBR Threats S&T Capabilities. As described above, the analysis is based on this *assumption*: a search of the specific keywords in the listed repositories and a search for 6 years represent a sufficiently representative search of published reports for the present pilot project.

† Six levels of impact were previously documented and contextualized in a Zachman Architecture Framework, as follows:

1. *TACTICAL*: At worker's perspective
2. *TACTICAL*: Component level at S&T performer's perspective (i.e., single study paper)
3. *OPERATIONAL*: Physics level at engineer's perspective (i.e., literature review)
4. *OPERATIONAL*: System logic at architect's perspective (i.e., integration of S&T, systems and capability)
5. *STRATEGIC*: Business concepts at S&T executive perspective (i.e., way ahead)
6. *STRATEGIC*: Scope concepts at stakeholder's perspective (i.e., formal S&T advice to senior officer)

Framework, each manuscript was assessed for *Who* (all authors) does *What*, *Where* (all listed organizations), *When*, *How*, *Why*, and at *What Level* (levels 1–6 of impact[†]) (Vallerand et al., 2016).

The approach interrogates the *messy data* along the *contextualized* fields of the Zachman Framework, and then, the SNA provides a visualization of the data analysis with various network measurements.

Results

The Centre for Security Science Programs and DRDC Programs have used various CoPs to generate new essential knowledge and advice to start to close national safety and security gaps in Canada for many years. Although Defense S&T Capabilities have been looked at in some detail in the past, presently, there is little information available to support the high level of interest in conceptualizing ways to mobilize the best *external* minds of the nation to tackle difficult problems in community. The approach used to identify this community included mining of S&T Capability through the lens of the Zachman Framework and then analyzing these data via a sociomatrix. Sociomatrices are adjacency matrices for graphs, and they become the foundation piece for the visual analytics through graphical theoretic notation.

The total volume of how each S&T Capability Community documents its work is comparable, since it varies from 34 in personnel Chemical, Biological, and Radiological (CBR) Protection; 32 in Blast Protection and Injury; 39 in Military Medicine; and 31 in Medical Countermeasures (MCM) against CBR threats (Figure 4.3a).[*] The proportion of DRDC's own publications versus that associated with the Canadian ecosystem (excluding the international publications not connected to DRDC) shows that while DRDC publications in Military Medicine represented 18% of the Canadian total, as expected for an *Access* type of S&T Capability, a very high proportion of DRDC documents (77%) was found for the MCM against CBR Community, a

---

[*] An additional list of 20, 180, 336, and 80 international reports (non-connected to DRDC) were found in S&T Capabilities 4.1, 4.2, 4.4, and 4.5, respectively, but are not shown here. Data shown represent the population, not samples of the defined population.

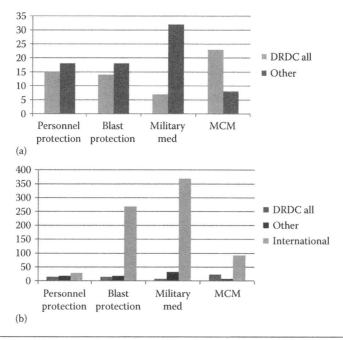

(a)

(b)

Figure 4.3 S&T Capability versus publications published/study period: (a) internal (DRDC) versus external in Canada and (b) internal (DRDC) versus external in Canada and international.

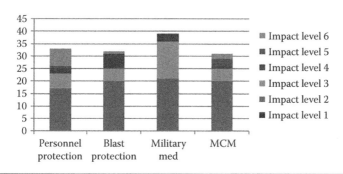

Figure 4.4 Impact levels for the publications for each S&T Capability in Canada.

domain deeply associated with the *Build* mode, whereas both Personnel CBR Protection and Blast Protection S&T Capabilities were at 44%. Figure 4.3b highlights the knowledge generation associated with the international S&T contributions across the domains. Figure 4.4 examines the (national) impact level of the work being documented by each community.

From the Zachman Framework, a network analysis was conducted across the various S&T domains to explicitly examine and visualize the *Who* and *Where*. The SNA analysis of Personnel Protection, as alluded to in Figure 4.3, shows a small international footprint. The SNA illustrated the lack of connectivity between national and international contributions, thereby supporting the opportunity for behavior change to improve connectivity and leverage distributed innovation. The SNA analysis of *MCM against CBR Threats*, as an example reveals a highly DRDC-centralized (i.e., not distributed) network of practitioners, as shown by its SNA visualization and its imposing *degree of centrality* metric (Figure 4.5a and b). Of note are the contribution of

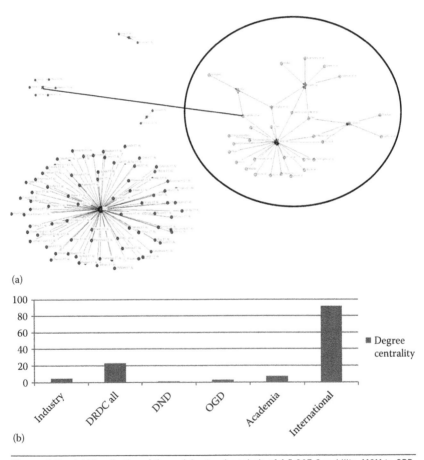

(a)

(b)

Figure 4.5 (a) Visualization of the social network analysis of 4.5 S&T Capability: MCM to CBR, and (b) visualization of its related degree of centrality (immediately above).

the international knowledge generation (outside the blue circle) and its lack of connectivity to the national contributions (inside the blue circle).

At the national level, Blast Protection Injury shows a bi-polar degree of centrality between DRDC and academia (Figure 4.6a and b), as well as the connectivity to the highly clustered node (international). It also shows very little connectivity with internationals.

Military Medicine displays the strongest degree of centrality not with DRDC or academia but with DND, Canadian forces health services (CFHS) (surgeon general) in particular (Figure 4.7a and b). Of note is the highly centralized cluster with connectivity to the national nodes, with only some connectivity with internationals.

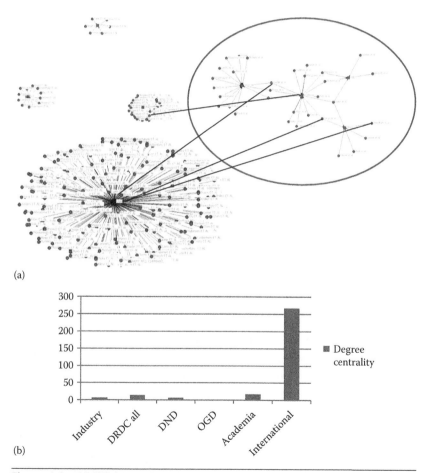

Figure 4.6   (a) SNA degree of centrality of 4.2 S&T Capability: Blast Protection Injury, and (b) visualization of its related degree of centrality (immediately above).

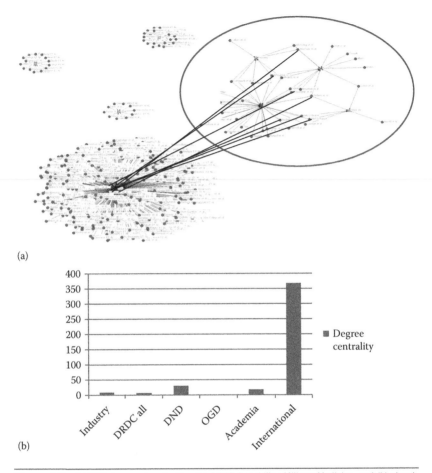

(a)

(b)

Figure 4.7   (a) SNA degree of centrality of 4.4 S&T Capability: Military Medicine, and (b) visualization of its related degree of centrality (immediately above).

It is suggested that the value in the present analysis maybe associated with making sense of voluminous (*messy*) data and supports reflective practices (Masys et al., 2014). For instance, is the present *as-is* posture, *now visible*, optimal or sufficient for the *to-be* S&T Capability? Additional questions could be as follows. Could the publication production found in Personnel CBR Protection (Figure 4.2) be improved by formally documenting CBR memorandum of understanding (MOU) reports from their related international CBR MOU Working Groups? Could the Military Medicine and Blast Protection Communities benefit from ensuring that as their tactical evidence is documented, then commensurate strategic advice (Figure 4.4) is given at an expected higher rate? Could the Personnel CBR Protection S&T Capability Community benefit from greater formal linkages with academia and royal military college (RMC) in particular, an important SNA pole with limited linkages back to DRDC? Is there an advantage to be gained by the MCM Community in developing greater linkages with any other S&T practitioners in Canada, including the International CBR MOU nations, by documenting their CBR MOU reports from the MCM Consortium Working Group? How can the S&T Community leverage the international contributions?

Reflective Practices

Big *messy* data analysis within the dynamic security landscape and supporting S&T problem framing and solution space call for *reflective practices* stemming from the Zachman and SNA analyses. As described in Masys et al. (2014), individual reflection resonates with the concept of *sense making* in organizations (Weick, 1995) that requires *interpretation* (Weick, 1995, p. 13). Interpretation is influenced by people's belief and mental models. According to Weick (1995, p. 15), sense making has a *strong reflexive quality* to the process of interpretation because "people make sense of things by seeing a world on which they already imposed what they believe." In this dynamic and complex security landscape, reflective practices thus can help avoid overconfidence through a generative learning approach.

"The value added by examining the big 'messy' data through the Zachman and SNA approaches is to facilitate *a focused process* for reflection" (Reynolds and Vince, 2004, p. 11) on the business of innovation and impact. Regarding interdisciplinary S&T, we ask the following questions:

1. How do I ensure the presence of S&T that crosses boundaries to potentially trigger *leap ahead innovation*, at least in big problem spaces?

2. Are my organization's actions (behaviors) and transactions aligned with strategic outcomes that the organization wants to achieve, and am I using the right *view* or *lens* to see the required course of action or course correction to get there, if any?

Reflective practice at the organizational level allows members to "... critically evaluate their own thinking, but also, to investigate the shared, collective assumptions and expectations, as well as the institutionalized rules and routines" (Hilden and Tikkamaki, 2013). To support the questions earlier, the messy data Zachman/Network analysis approach revealed insights and reflections across the following (Figure 4.8):

- Strategic positioning.
  - What are the defense and security priorities, and how do we leverage the distributed S&T innovation system?
- S&T management practices.
  - How do we facilitate greater collaboration across communities of practice (CoPs)?
- Human resources.
  - Where does the S&T expertise exist, and how do I leverage it? How do I grow it?
- Leadership and culture.
  - What are the leadership and cultural conditions that allow S&T innovation networks to thrive?

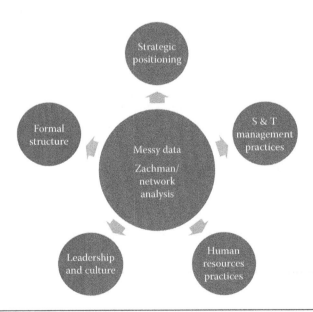

Figure 4.8 Supporting reflective practices from Zachman/network analysis. (From Cross, R., and Parker, A., *The Hidden Power of Social Networks: Understanding How Work Really Gets Done in Organizations*, Harvard Business Press, Boston, MA, p. 117, 2004.)

- Formal structure.
  - How do I establish the boundaries and decision rights to encourage innovation?

In support of a strategic framing of the S&T analysis, reflection creates an opportunity to share, compare, and explore mental models, thus opening up consideration of a variety of possibilities. This learning is rooted in an organization's ability to frame and then reframe and emerges from reflective practices. This is about being cognizant of organizational paradigms, mindsets, and mental models that shape decision making. Chermack and Nimon (2013, p. 816) argue that "most critical is the ability to change ones" mental model, in order to view the future of an organization through a new lens. Such reflective practice requires dialogue and conversation about strategic issues that decision makers are facing (Chermack, 2011; Georgantzas and Acar, 1995; Schwartz, 1991; van der Heijden, 1997, 2005; Wack, 1985a). The Zachman Framework and Network Analysis presents the 360° vision to help facilitate the strategic conversation and reflective practices, thereby shaping S&T investment and collaborative networks supporting innovation. Future research efforts look to exploit the *When* dimension of the Zachman Framework to facilitate trend analysis regarding innovation.

Conclusion

The defense, security, and safety landscape is a complex and dynamic environment. Addressing this dynamic landscape from an S&T perspective is a matter of understanding and leveraging the S&T capabilities to close gaps and to provide advice, innovative solutions, and support across the defense, security, and safety landscape. This *pilot project* addresses *S&T Situational Awareness* (Vallerand et al., 2016) in the health sciences sector within the S&T Capability CoP. With the evidence presented, it is suggested that combining a Zachman Architecture Framework analysis (Zachman, 2003) with a well-documented SNA (Masys, 2014, 2016) enabled novel visualization to actually *see* otherwise-invisible *360° views* of each S&T Capability. Such data analysis then triggered the formulation of new questions to better inform related discussions with decision makers, facilitating dialogue across the following: strategic positioning, S&T management practices, human resources practices, leadership and culture, and formal structure. It is suggested that combining this set of twin analyses can easily be applied and be of value to any other scientific domain. The power of the Zachman analysis and SNA appears to be in facilitating *reflective practices*. It forces one to challenge one's assumptions and mental models, as it pertains to the S&T that we are providing, and thereby ask the questions that emerge from the visualizations. Interrogating the big *messy* data, the Zachman Framework and SNA analyses generated new visualizations of the S&T Capabilities; the questions that need to be raised may not be related to what the *as-is* S&T Capability is right now. The questions should rather be: what should it look like *going forward*, and is there room to potentially consider a change in behavior, as discussed earlier and as appropriate, to affect the desired *to-be* posture of S&T Capabilities?

Acknowledgments

This manuscript was generated through equal authorship of all three coauthors.

References

Canadian Government Executive Magazine. (2015) Big data analytics delivers actionable intelligence. March 30, 2015. http://canadiangovernment executive.ca/big-data-analytics-delivers-actionable-intelligence/.

Chermack, T.J. (2011) *Scenario Planning in Organizations: How to Create, Use, and Assess Scenarios*, CA: Berrett-Koehler Publishers.

Chermack, T.J., and Nimon, K. (2013) Drivers and outcomes of scenario planning: A canonical correlation analysis. *European Journal of Training and Development* 37(9): 811–834.

Comeau, P. et al. (2015) *S&T Capability Assessment Methodology*. DRDC-RDDC-2016-L001.

Cross, R., and Parker, A. (2004) *The Hidden Power of Social Networks: Understanding How Work Really Gets Done in Organizations*. Boston, MA: Harvard Business Press.

Defence Research and Development Canada (DRDC). (2014) Defence and security S&T strategy. http://www.drdc-rddc.gc.ca/assets/DRDC_Internet/docs/en/ST-Strategy.pdf, accessed September 20, 2016.

Georgantzas, N.C. and Acar, W. (1995) *Scenario-driven Planning: Learning to Manage Strategic Uncertainty*, Westport, CT: Quorum Books.

Gunduz-Oguducu, S., and Etaner-Uyar, A.S. (2014) *Social Networks: Analysis and Case Studies*. Berlin, Germany: Springer.

Hilden, S., and Tikkamaki, K. (2013) Reflective practice as a fuel for organizational learning. *Administrative Sciences* 3: 76–95.

Masys, A.J. (ed.) (2014) *Networks and Network Analysis for Defence and Security*. Berlin, Germany: Springer.

Masys, A.J. (ed.) (2016) *Exploring the Security Landscape: Non-traditional Security Challenges*. Berlin, Germany: Springer.

Masys, A.J., Ray-Bennett, N., Shiroshita, H., and Jackson, P. (2014) High impact/low frequency extreme events: Enabling reflection and resilience in a hyper-connected world. *4th International Conference on Building Resilience*, September 8–11, 2014, Salford Quays. Procedia Economics and Finance 18: 772–779.

Reynolds, M., and Vince, R. (2004) Organizing reflection: An introduction. In: Organizing Reflection. Reynolds, M., and Vince, R. (eds.). Hampshire: Ashgate Publishing.

Schwartz, P. (1991) *The Art of the Long View*. New York: Doubleday.

van der Heijden, K. (1997) *Scenarios: The Art of Strategic Conversation*. New York: John Wiley & Sons.

van der Heijden, K. (2005) *Scenarios: The Art of Strategic Conversation*. 2nd ed., New York: John Wiley & Sons.

Vallerand, A.L., Masys, A., and Geling, G. (2016) *S&T Capability Visualization through Zachman Architecture Framework*. Ottawa, Canada: DRDC. DRDC-RDDC-2016-L045.

Wack, P. (1985a) *Scenarios: shooting the rapids*, Harvard Business Review, Vol.63: pp. 139–150.

Wasserman, S., and Faust, K. (1994) *Social Network Analysis: Methods and Applications*. New York: Cambridge University Press.

Weick, K.E. (1995) *Sensemaking in Organizations*. London: Sage Publications.

Zachman, J.A. (2003) The Zachman Framework: A primer for enterprise engineering and manufacturing. http://www.zachmaninternational.com, accessed February 8, 2016.

5

Big Data Analytics and Public Bus Transportation Systems in China

A Strategic Intelligence Approach Based on Knowledge and Risk Management

EDUARDO RODRIGUEZ

Contents

Introduction

Strategic intelligence (Maccoby 2015) in this chapter is based on the appropriate use of risk and knowledge management. During the last 10 years, the concept of Big Data, referring to structured and unstructured data characterized by high volume, velocity, and variety, has emerged (Chen et al., 2012; McAfee and Brynjolfsson 2012). Furthermore, devices that provide data are a common factor in the world of Big Data Goes (2014). In this paper, the Big Data Analytics (BDA) concepts are illustrated using structured data generated by a sensor installed on the buses. The case illustration is presented through two aspects: first, the transformation of raw data to usable data, and second, reflections about the development of the BDA process.

There is not much written about relationships between knowledge and risk management. Rodriguez and Edwards (2014) indicate the existence of relationships between knowledge management variables and risk control. Mainly, they indicate how knowledge positively affects the risk control process. The BDA process (Pries and Dunnigan 2015) can be viewed as part of strategic intelligence development in organizations. This is because the BDA process creates knowledge and therefore augments intelligence, allowing managers to deal effectively with risk. In particular, strategic risks (McPhee 2014) can be analyzed based on the variation of events or conditions internal or external to the organizations. In the context of public bus transportation systems (PBTS), strategic risk refers to the variation in efficiency and effectiveness of operations of the PBTS that are designed to enable sustainable transportation in cities. The BDA process, therefore, should be enacted within a framework that is conscious of the strategic objectives, the ways in which knowledge can be generated and distributed within the organization, and the decision-support models involved in converting analysis to action.

The BDA process calls for data to be gathered from operational activities (i.e., the driver's habits during service delivery). These data are then aggregated and analyzed to identify variance from expected performance objectives and therefore point to either strategic or operational improvement strategies that can be enacted to achieve the strategic objectives of a PBTS. This case study describes how sensor data allow the identification of driver's actions during the continuous execution of his work. It is a situation where the use of devices connected to decision-support systems (i.e., the so-called Internet of Things [IoT]) provides data to discover improvement opportunities. Although there is a wealth of data gathered, this case study addresses only driver's skillsets associated with the attributes of the road, machine performance, routes, and schedule.

In summary, the main concept is that BDA is a means of generating knowledge, and the use of BDA requires appropriate information systems (decision support, and so on). The collection and analysis of data generate knowledge that, when aligned with the organization's strategic objectives and management control systems, permits operational and/or strategic changes to help the organization deliver on its strategic objectives. In this case, a key preoccupation for managers of the PBTS is variance from expected targets, which can be interpreted as strategic risk. When viewed from this holistic perspective, BDA drives better management control systems (Anthony and Govindarajan, 2007) for the PBTS and strategic intelligence improvement develops because the data help clarify the problem and potential solutions for decision makers. In this case, how can one be more efficient in fuel consumption to provide justification for further significant investments in hybrid buses?

Efficiency can result from the better use of the machine (the bus), which in turn comes from a more skilled group of drivers that gain experience in driving the hybrid buses in a more efficient way. The issue is to find where to improve and the specific steps involved in implementing improvement initiatives. The following sections provide an overview of the concept of strategic intelligence, followed by a description of a case study in which a BDA process is used to achieve a smarter PBTS based on the understanding of the relationship between driver's behaviors and fuel efficiency.

How to Improve Strategic Intelligence

The main steps for developing strategic intelligence are related to the development of capabilities to improve the management of knowledge, risk, and control systems (Marchand and Hykes 2007; Maccoby 2015). All of them require the creation of support systems in order to convert data into knowledge and actions.

Strategic intelligence is strengthened through the best use of knowledge and the understanding of risk factors that influence performance of a system (in this case, the PBTS). Knowledge is based on the analytics that derive meaning from the structured data that originate from sensors in the bus and that are subsequently managed by the information system. These data describe the driver's experience during the bus's journey, and the information system provides the foundation for analysis, capturing and transforming appropriate variables from the sensor's raw data.

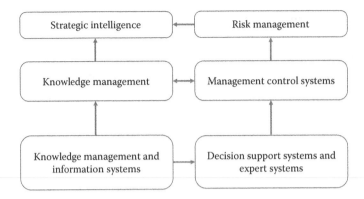

Figure 5.1   Connection of risk management, knowledge management, and management control systems.

Thus, strategic intelligence depends on the development of capabilities to capture and process data as well as to convert data into knowledge that informs both the management controls and risk management systems within an organization (Figure 5.1). Knowledge is the foundation for mitigation of risk, and analytics is a way to create knowledge. However, the BDA process should be done in such a way that it supports all other organizational processes that generate strategic intelligence.

Strategic Intelligence in Public Bus Transportation System

In general, in a PBTS, there are many related processes for improving strategic intelligence. A key starting point is an understanding of the business. Following Abell's three-dimensional business definition model (Abell 1980), we note that the buses serve a number of key customer segments, not only the riders but also society in general through the notion of sustainability. The issue here is that the buses should use the electric system more than the fuel-based engines. Further, customers themselves have specific needs for the bus to be on time, to be driven safely, and so on. Finally, the technology dimension includes not only the technical aspects of the PBTS but also the management processes involved in scheduling, staffing, and overall control of the processes involved in transporting passengers. Taking this three-dimensional perspective suggests that, for example, the ticketing process can affect PBTS performance in the same way as a malfunctioning bus or an impaired driver.

With this strategic view in mind, improving strategic intelligence in the PBTS requires development of an efficiency-sustainability measurement system that recognizes all three dimensions of the PBTS business definition. This measurement system could include variables such as schedule, timing, accommodation, stops, costs, pricing, routes, and budget. In addition, many stakeholders (customers, drivers, other vehicles, society, and so on) and their needs could be considered in defining goals to achieve in the PBTS enhancements.

Furthermore, once these general goals are defined, there is a need to review points of solution to PBTS business processes, such as payment methods, bus renewal, training of bus drivers, road adjustments, technology adjustments as global positioning system (GPS)/geographic information system (GIS)-based driving practice, and bus design adjustments. Some examples of potential enhancements include the following:

- Openness of service personnel to change
- Organizational structure
- Budgeting
- Divisions' alignment in goals and processes
- Definition of revenue centers
- Definition of expense centers
- Definition of discretionary centers
- Performance evaluation system—customers, internal and external
- Transfer pricing, and so on

However, not all of these factors can be reviewed in this chapter, and the concentration is therefore on using the BDA process for improving the human–machine relationship in search of higher performance (Figure 5.2). More specifically, in terms of hybrid buses, synchronization and use of the acceleration function, breaking, and speed influence the exchange between the use of electric (clean) energy and the bus's fuel-based engine. Therefore, the sustainability aspect, a key goal of the use of the PBTS in the first place, is an important element to be considered.

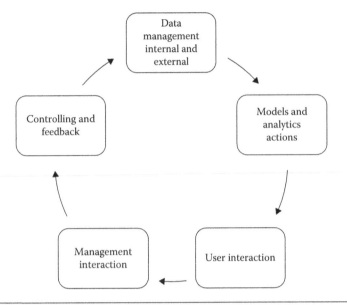

Figure 5.2   Continuous process to create value from data.

The BDA process supports the creation of analytic capabilities to address the holistic view of what the PBTS is supposed to accomplish. The information system, a key aspect of the *technology* dimension according to Abell's model (in particular, decision support systems and analytics capabilities), is an important organizational element. So too is the consideration of external factors, for example, benchmarking of public transportation operators (Geerlings et al. 2006; Hilmola 2011). The connections of benchmarks and other external independent reviews of factors such as government's needs and user and driver requirements (Lan and Kuo 2003; Tse et al. 2006; Hajiamiri and Wachs 2010; Krutilla and Graham 2012) are also inputs for the BDA process.

Big Data Process

Given that the data used in the case study are coming from sensors (IoT) installed on the buses, the use of BDA is associated with the concept of Analytics of Things (AoT). Davenport (2014) argues that,

"The AoT term points out that IoT devices generate a lot of data, and that data must be analyzed to be useful. It also suggests that analytics are necessary to make connected devices smart and for them to take intelligent action. Connection, on the other hand, isn't required for intelligent action."

The BDA process in this context is in itself a human–machine interactive approach, in which the sensors transmit data that are analyzed by humans, who then make decisions about how to adjust the PBTS. In some situations, the sensors themselves can be programmed to make adjustments in real time. However, this programming also requires human intervention and monitoring. Therefore, the overall BDA process in this case includes (1) problem definition; (2) data capture and organization; (3) data exploration; (4) interpretation of results; and (5) knowledge transfer, application, and feedback. In some cases, human intervention in terms of scheduling or training might be needed. In other cases, technical adjustments to the buses might be required.

Problem Definition

Problem definition calls for developing an appropriate identification of the specific questions to explore: roads, routes, loops, fuel cycles, and so on. For example, in Figure 5.3, we see the fuel consumption graphs for five buses on the same route. Fuel use is an important consideration for both efficiency and sustainability goals. Therefore, in this stage, the complete scope and boundaries need to be clear to formulate questions and answers, such as the following:

- What are the relationships between driving skillsets/practice/ knowledge variables and the plug-in hybrid bus performance variables?
- What are the factors affecting the variance of the expected/ planned results of the system?
- Is it possible to classify in groups the performance of the plug-in hybrid system operation?

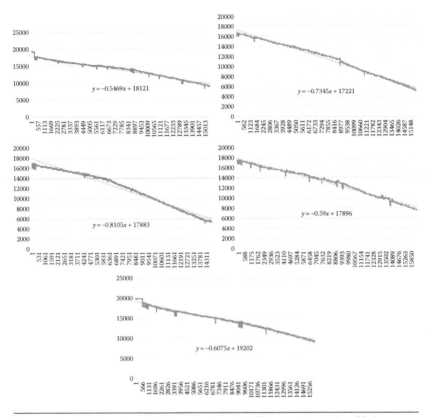

Figure 5.3   One bus route and five buses to observe the differences in variation of fuel consumption. Five buses with the same road, different rates of fuel consumption, same days. Possible factors, among many, influencing the changes of the rate of fuel consumption: Time/traffic and driverskills.

Data Capture and Organization

Data management includes a series of steps to ensure that the right variables are available for analysis:

Data Collection   Capture and manage test data, create training data for models, and manage current real-time data. A number of substeps were necessary at this stage.

- *Defining the categories of data needed*: Five categories were identified, which included GPS data, battery system, electromotor system, bus control system, and engine systems. From these data, some fields were used to define variables representing bus performance and driver's skills such as bus performance–related variables (battery charge by regenerative braking and compressed natural gas (CNG)-consuming efficiency (CNG is the fuel, compressed natural gas). This is a performance indicator variable defined as a combination of the raw data CNG% pressure, output voltage and current of the power battery, and hybrid status. A cycle is defined from the highest pressure level to the minimum level. This cycle includes many route loops, and there are 30 cycles per month for each bus. A representation of CNG pressure cycle and the loops is shown in Figure 5.3 for various buses, indicating the changes on the slope of the consumption.

- *Identifying the buses and routes to be studied*: Two types of data of bus routes were used: one with no extreme changes in the orography, and another with high changes in the orography. A month of data was selected to isolate the effects of weather and use of the bus and driver resources. In particular, the time frames involved had no air conditioning use and no winter conditions.
- *Defining zones*: Including differentiation among routes, initial and final points of the route, and location of the refuel points.

Data Cleansing Here, the job is to define the rules for cleaning data. This is a crucial aspect in this research because of the Big Data characteristics of the data. Many records are not useful for the analysis. Then, it is important to clarify which data points to use and which ones to discard. The substeps involved are discussed as follows.

Preparing Data This is to pass from raw data to data that can be used in the analytics process. In this case, these data include GPS data and data generated by the internal bus control system.

Defining Variables (see the text box for examples) Creation of new variables describing the driver's skills: These variables were defined as bivariate combinations and selected from some thresholds with *normal* and *abnormal* characteristics. (See appendix for the variable labels, where normal = 0 and abnormal = 1.) By using quintiles and combinations of two raw data variables, it was possible to create new variables.

DEFINING VARIABLES

1. Variable to review the engine rotation rate and bus speed. *Rotspeed* = 1: rank_g27 (rank in front of the variable means that the original variables were ranked, and then, ranks were used in the analysis) is equal to 3 or 4 and rank_g9 is equal to 0 or 1.
2. Variable to review the bus speed and accelerator pedal use. *Ecusacped* = 1: rank_g9 is equal to 0 or 1 and rank_g14 is equal to 3 or 4, or rank_g9 is equal to 3 or 4 and rank_g14 is equal to 0 or 1.
3. Variable associating bus speed and brake use. *Ecusbr* = 1: rank_g9 is equal to 4 and g12 is equal to 1.
4. Variable associating bus speed and door status. *Ecusdo* = 1: rank_g9 is equal to 4 and g23 is equal to 1,2,3,6.
5. Variable associating speed and gear status. *Ecusge* = 1: rank_g9 is equal to 0 or 1 and g13 is equal to 4,5,6, or rank_g9 is equal to 3 or 4 and g13 is equal to 1,2,3.

Identifying Missing Data   Identification of records without complete data: no GPS data, internal system data, or any other data anomalies.

Data Exploration

This step includes performing exploratory and data mining analyses with raw data and preparing usable data. This is a recursive process in data organization and preparation. Some of the analytics steps will identify conditions for data changes as well. This means that the exploration of test models will highlight issues in the data that require further cleaning or transformation. For instance, the use of GPS data can be affected by signal interruption and outliers. Basic statistics analysis and clustering (Figure 5.4) contribute to improving the data used in the final analysis.

Once data are ready to use, a set of models (mathematical and statistical) can be tested and observed in terms of performance, comparing outputs, and reviewing the pros and cons of using those models.

Descriptive with some clusters

g1	Weekday												
	1		2		3		4		5		6		7
	ratiog18 Mean		ratiog18 Mean		ratiog18 Mean		ratiog18 Mean		ratiog18 Mean		ratiog18 Mean		ratiog18 Mean
20661	0.7		0.7		0.69		0.67		0.69		0.68		0.67
20662	0.58		0.62		0.61		0.62		0.62		0.61		0.6
20663	0.7		0.7		0.7		0.69		0.69		0.7		0.71
20664	0.66		0.69		0.68		0.65		0.66		0.66		0.67
20665	0.68		0.7		0.71		0.68		0.69		0.67		0.68
20666	0.71		0.71		0.69		0.68		0.69		0.68		0.7
20668	0.69		0.7		0.7		0.67		0.66		0.65		0.67
20669	0.59		0.63		0.63		0.61		0.62		0.58		0.61
20670	0.63		0.65		0.63		0.62		0.61		0.64		0.6
20671	0.65		0.65		0.66		0.63		0.64		0.65		0.65
20672	0.59		0.56		0.54		0.53		0.53		0.59		0.57
20673	0.59		0.61		0.61		0.6		0.64		0.6		0.63
20674	0.7		0.71		0.71		0.7		0.7		0.72		0.69
20675	0.63		0.65		0.62		0.61		0.64		0.67		0.64
20676	0.66		0.68		0.68		0.69		0.68		0.67		0.66
20677	0.63		0.67		0.66		0.66		0.64		0.6		0.67
20678	0.69		0.68		0.7		0.7		0.67		0.68		0.65
20679	0.7		0.67		0.67		0.65		0.66		0.68		0.66
20680	0.64		0.67		0.67		0.67		0.67		0.67		0.66
20681	0.6		0.61		0.62		0.62		0.62		0.59		0.59
20682	0.6		0.63		0.56		0.56		0.6		0.6		0.61
20683	0.68		0.71		0.68		0.66		0.68		0.7		0.69
20684	0.59		0.56		0.63		0.6		0.62		0.61		0.61
20685	0.67		0.68		0.71		0.67		0.69		0.7		0.69
20686	0.65		0.65		0.66		0.61		0.67		0.64		0.65
20688			0.79		0.87		0.83		0.65		0.83		.
20689	0.64		0.64		0.65		0.6		0.64		0.64		0.68
20690	0.6		0.58		0.57		0.55		0.56		0.56		0.56

Cluster	Cluster means					
	rank_g14	rank_g32	rank_g27	rank_g25	rank_ratiog18	rank_g10
1	0.416615	0.93764998	0.71311781	0.512100957	1.032531729	0.723973621
2	0.411797771	3.00490337	2.66867299	1.465394281	3.178910992	2.678752899
3	0.940150996	0.55837017	1.55154577	2.559685554	3.04117995	1.554332192
4	1.651363942	3.27676934	0.254406812	0.411595386	1.508532671	0.254164935
5	2.844172037	2.63355789	3.55013903	2.631600883	0.803867788	3.546949736
6	3.393553167	2.81528569	1.61756857	3.093563841	2.844955914	1.606621439
7	3.430377859	0.82584394	1.64987722	2.990920302	0.854473576	1.63995891
8	2.623952742	1.48409645	3.49895018	3.071160697	3.01692949	3.495626241
9	0.426749048	2.95192105	2.93362104	2.644710413	0.716922211	2.938955307
10	1.657968216	0.92051883	0.28873418	0.432264857	3.227580926	0.288955562

Data observation by day and cluster member's identification

Figure 5.4 The BDA process needs the understanding of groups of buses according to their attributes.

The model identification that is appropriate for the problem solution depends on the type of model as descriptive, predictive, or prescriptive. In this particular case study, the important models are descriptive and predictive ones: descriptive because of the need of finding the variables' attributes and their combinations to define driver's/buses/road/routes profiles, and predictive because of the need of classifying drivers and machines according to the practice and results in PBTS efficiency. In this case study, logistic regression was used. The basic description is given in the section *Interpretation of Results*, which complements the visualization of variable statistics across buses, time, and routes. In the section *Interpretation of Results*, there is an illustration of using basic statistic metrics in a way that they can offer insights about the way to improve driver's skillsets and fuel consumption.

Interpretation of Results

The use of descriptive statistics and visualization helps in the definition of the measurement system for evaluating and controlling variations in metrics. The variations, as shown in Figures 5.5a and b and 5.6, can be a representation of risks just by observing the variation noted in the buses. Risks in this case are associated with the variation that affects the overall objectives of the PBTS system in terms of sustainability and fuel consumption.

Figure 5.5a represents the correlation coefficients between fuel consumption and the driver's skill variables taken for the whole set of buses. The observation is for all buses on the same route and during the same window of time. The observations suggest that buses have different performance results. The correlation coefficients are not stable when the whole set of buses is observed. This is a potential point to start in reducing the variability of the metric. This presentation of correlation coefficients variability indicates the need for actions in the PBTS to align the development of driver's skills and the common variables across buses (machines).

The review of principal components (Figure 5.5b) indicates through the biplots how the variables are related to the variance in the data. In this example, the biplots show less than 50% of the variation and provide hints to search for reasons such as driver's skills and time factors that can modify the fuel consumption variation.

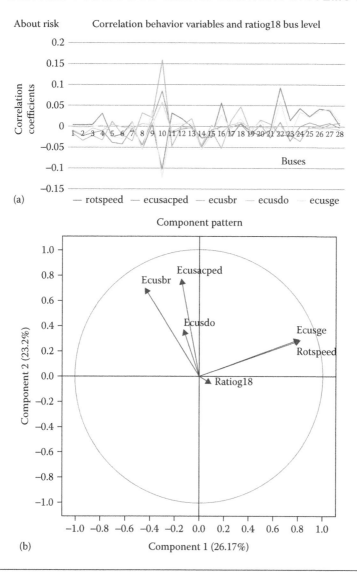

Figure 5.5 (a) Observation of the variability of correlation coefficients between driver's skills and fuel consumption for all buses. (b) Observation of the biplots in principal components.

Figure 5.6 provides an additional view of risk by using descriptive statistics. The variation of the means by buses for the variable *g_14* that corresponds to accelerator pedal use can be a metric to review in controlling the PBTS. The reason is that keeping the same route and days, the priority will be to find the reasons for variation in

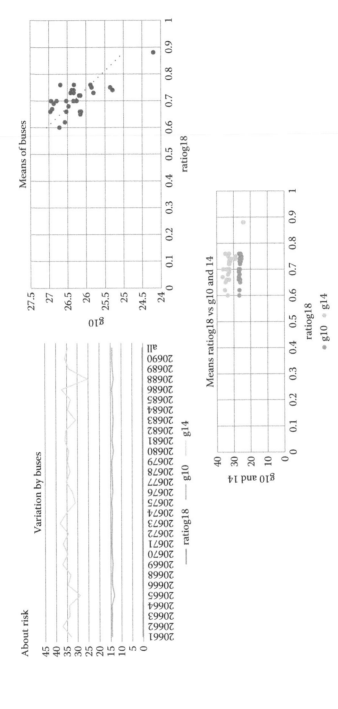

Figure 5.6 Observation of the variation of the means in variables related to fuel consumption.

(machine- and human-related) and the influence on fuel consumption. A graphical representation of fuel consumption means by buses against the variables acceleration pedal (g_14) and speed (g_10) identifies different groups of buses (in this case, different drivers and the same type of machine). This part of the BDA process provides some clues to investigate in depth and indicates further possible reasons for variation in fuel consumption.

Visualization and description are very important steps in BDA, but in most of the cases, they are not enough, and the BDA process requires more modeling support. The search for answers to business questions can use several methods and models through statistical and machine-learning (supervised-learning) algorithms/techniques for reviewing the classification based on fuel efficiency levels. One of these methods is logistic regression.

The first aspect is the need for variables adapted to the model use. The logistic regression model can take a bivariate variable created from the original g_18 fuel consumption and is called ratiog_18. Value 1 means that the ratio between the actual fuel consumption and the maximum (ratiog_18) is greater than 60% (4th and 5th quintiles), and value 0 means the complementary set. In this illustration, the *bi* coefficients are for 12 variables, indicating significance for all of these variables (human- and machine-related), except *rankg_27* and *rotspeed* (both machine-related). Moreover, it is important to review whether the resulting correlation coefficient is positive or negative because variables such as *ecusdo* suggest an inverse relationship to the log odds of being in one of the highest quintiles (i.e., more than 60%) of the ratiog_18.

The second aspect is the possible success and limitation of models. Figure 5.7 indicates the receiver operating characteristic (ROC) curve to interpret the classification capacity of the logistic regression model applied to the PBTS data. The classification is not very clear yet, as the ROC curve indicates being close to the diagonal (a naive classification). In the BDA process, it is required to improve the model performance through definition of new variables, inclusion of new variables, or search of better models. Some options for classification improvement can be to use different raw (original) variables, to define variables related to the human skills in a different way, and, possibly, to review the use of partitioned data according to factors such as hours of service and weekdays. In particular, in this example, the BDA requires the

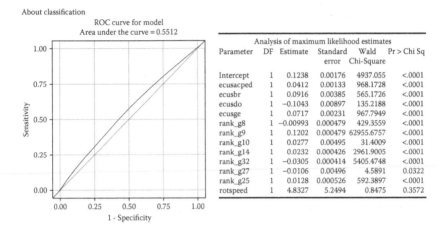

About classification

Analysis of maximum likelihood estimates					
Parameter	DF	Estimate	Standard error	Wald Chi-Square	Pr > Chi Sq
Intercept	1	0.1238	0.00176	4937.055	<.0001
ecusacped	1	0.0412	0.00133	968.1728	<.0001
ecusbr	1	0.0916	0.00385	565.1726	<.0001
ecusdo	1	−0.1043	0.00897	135.2188	<.0001
ecusge	1	0.0717	0.00231	967.7949	<.0001
rank_g8	1	−0.00993	0.000479	429.3559	<.0001
rank_g9	1	0.1202	0.000479	62955.6757	<.0001
rank_g10	1	0.0277	0.00495	31.4009	<.0001
rank_g14	1	0.0232	0.000426	2961.9005	<.0001
rank_g32	1	−0.0305	0.000414	5405.4748	<.0001
rank_g27	1	−0.0106	0.00496	4.5891	0.0322
rank_g25	1	0.0128	0.000526	592.3897	<.0001
rotspeed	1	4.8327	5.2494	0.8475	0.3572

The dependent variable is a bivariate of ratiog18 upper 60% = 1 and 0 lower

Figure 5.7   Presentation of classification ROC and regression coefficients.

search for logistic model results through methods such as stepwise method to obtain the appropriate selection of significant variables.

Knowledge Transfer, Application, and Feedback

Finally, going back to Figure 5.1, a knowledge management system (KMS) for strategic intelligence improvement is required. The KMS, including the BDA process, is designed to enable stakeholders to use the created knowledge. This calls for a process of knowledge transfer related to enhancements and development of the PBTS. Every step in the BDA process requires a feedback review around metrics design, conceptualization, and understanding of the model's outcomes.

Moreover, in the PBTS, the creation of time series with performance indicators leads to the analysis of new data (the values of the metrics). This analysis is performed using time series techniques in order to forecast PBTS results or to use the value of the metrics as input for Monte Carlo simulation process in the PBTS.

In summary, in these sections, the BDA process has been reviewed to put in evidence the value of improving strategic intelligence in PBTS. Strategic intelligence improvement has been described based on achieving a better understanding of areas to gain efficiency and make the PBTS sustainable. The review focused on defining variables related to drivers' skills that can affect efficiency. The logic behind this is that, possibly, better knowledge of driver in interaction with the machine (in particular, these hybrid buses) can lead to improved fuel consumption. This enhancement will be on reduction in fuel volume (cost related) and, at the same time, an increment in the use of clean energy.

Final Remarks

The PBTS can be improved through an understanding of the interaction of the human and machine in order to increase efficiency. The level of efficiency improvement required depends on defining the appropriate benchmarks for operating the system and reducing variability (Figure 5.3). The path of improvement runs through the information system developed for managing data from sensors on the buses. Moreover, KMS and management control systems are indicated as means to aid interpretation of the results, thereby converting data into actions.

The case helps demonstrate that building strategic intelligence though the BDA process starts with a clear definition of the problem and a selection of the path that leads to corporate performance improvement. There are many information systems that can be designed in a PBTS, each one with different levels of complexity. However, the focus on information systems to develop BDA capabilities is part of creating knowledge (Davenport and Harris, 2007) that will lead to control risk, finding opportunities, and enabling the implementation of strategies. The BDA process calls for significant effort on the definition, collection, and cleaning of the required data according to the problem that has been defined. The subsequent analysis generates knowledge that needs to be transferred, in order to develop solutions and actions.

With regard to strategic risk, the expectation is that with a better BDA process, there is an improvement in how to define objectives in the organization and control variability of the expected results. The point is that BDA solutions should not be viewed in isolation of other management processes in the organization, because the analytics are often only one part of an overall improvement process.

Appendix

LABEL1	LABEL2	DESCRIPTION
busid	G_1	Bus identification
time	G_2	Time of the record
gpslong	G_3	GPS_longitude
gpslat	G_4	GPS_latitude
gpssp	G_5	GPS_Speed
gpsalt	G_6	GPS_altitude
gpsdir	G_7	GPS_Direction
gpsackm	G_8	GPS_Accumulation
ecuspeed	G_10	ecu speed (speed control)
accumkm	G_9	Accumulated KM
parbre	G_11	Parking brake
brake	G_12	Brake
gear	G_13	Gear
accped	G_14	Acceleration pedal
hybst	G_15	Hybrid status
prefbrakair	G_16	Pressure of front brake air bottle
prerbrakair	G_17	Pressure of rear brake air bottle
precng	G_18	Pressure of CNG bottle
voltbat	G_19	Voltage of 24V storage battery
prengoil	G_20	Pressure of engine oil
temengcool	G_21	Temperature of engine coolant
ligstat	G_22	Light status
doorst	G_23	Door status
temelectmot	G_24	Temperature of electrometer
electrotrat	G_25	Electrometer rotation rate
current	G_26	Current
enginrotrat	G_27	Engine rotation rate
tempinver	G_28	Temperature of inventor
voltage	G_29	Voltage
maxvoltsingbat	G_30	Max voltage of single battery
minvoltsingbat	G_31	Min voltage of single battery
soc%	G_32	SOC "%"
maxtempbat	G_33	MAX temperature of battery
mintempbat	G_34	MIN temperature of battery
x1	G_35	N/A
x2	G_36	N/A
maxpochar	G_37	Max power of charge
maxpodisch	G_38	Max power of discharge
insolrisipo	G_39	Insulation of resistance of positive electrode

(Continued)

LABEL1	LABEL2	DESCRIPTION
insolrisineg	G_40	Insulation of resistance of negative electrode
tempengair	G_41	Temperature of engine air admission
hcumalfunc	G_42	HCU_Malfunction Code
hcuparam	G_43	HCU_Parameter
tcumalfunc	G_44	TCU_Malfunction Code
tcutcuparam	G_45	TCU_Parameter
chargetstat	G_46	Charge status

References

Abell D. 1980. *Defining the Business: The Starting Point of Strategic Planning.* Englewood Cliffs, NJ: Prentice Hall.

Anthony R, Govindarajan V. 2007. *Management Control Systems.* Boston, MA: Irwin.

Chen H, *Chiang RHL, Storey VC.* 2012. Business intelligence and analytics: From big data to big impact. MIS Quarterly, 36, 1165–1188.

Davenport TH, Harris JG. 2007. *Competing on Analytics: The New Science of Winning.* Boston, MA: Harvard Business School Review Press.

Davenport T. 2014. A predictive analytics primer. *Harvard Business Review,* September 2.

Geerlings H, Klementschitz R, Mulley C. 2006. Development of a methodology for benchmarking public transportation organisations: A practical tool based on an industry sound methodology. *Journal of Cleaner Production,* 14, 113–123.

Goes PB. 2014. Big data and IS research. *MIS Quarterly,* 38, iii–viii.

Hajiamiri S, Wachs M.2010. Hybrid electric vehicles and implications for transportation finance. *Public Works Management & Policy,* 15(2), 121–135.

Hilmola OP. 2011. Benchmarking efficiency of public passenger transport in larger cities. *Benchmarking: An International Journal,* 18(1), 23–41.

Krutilla K, Graham J. 2012. Are green vehicles worth the extra cost? The case of diesel-electric hybrid technology for urban delivery vehicles. *Journal of Policy Analysis and Management,* 31(3), 501–532.

Lan LW, Kuo AY. 2003. Modeling bus drivers' aberrant behaviors and the influences on fuel and maintenance costs. *Journal of Advanced Transportation,* 38(1), 93–113.

Maccoby M. 2015. *Strategic Intelligence: Conceptual Tools for Leading Change.* Oxford Scholarship Online.

Marchand D, Hykes A. 2007. *Leveraging What Your Company Really Knows: A Process View of Strategic Intelligence in Managing Strategic Intelligence: Techniques and Technologies,* edited by Xu M. Hershey, PA: IGI Publishing.

McAfee A, Brynjolfsson E. 2012. Big data: The management revolution. *Harvard Business Review*, 90, 60–68.

McPhee JE. 2014. *Mastering Strategic Risk: A Framework for Leading and Transforming Organizations*. Hoboken, NJ: John Wiley & Sons.

Pries KH, Dunnigan R. 2015. *Big Data Analytics: A Practical Guide for Managers*. Boca Raton, FL: Auerbach Publications.

Rodriguez E, Edwards J. 2014. Knowledge management in support of enterprise risk management. *International Journal of Knowledge Management (IJKM)*, 10(2), 43–61.

Tse JLM, Flin R, Mearns K. 2006. Bus driver well-being review: 50 years of research. *Transportation Research Part F*, 9, 89–114.

6

Government of India Prepares for Big Data Analytics Using Aadhaar Card Unique Identification System

NIKHIL VARMA AND RAJESH K. TYAGI

Contents

Introduction

The Government of India has several social and economic programs for its citizens. These programs aim to support the economically diverse population of 1.2 billion people on various aspects; however, the delivery of these programs has faced the issues of reach, time-lines, and loss of revenue related to misdirected social benefits payments. One significant problem was that the people belonging to marginalized and economically or socially disadvantaged sections of the society of India often did not have a robust and tamper-proof form of identity. The lack of a robust proof of identity also gave rise to several other issues such as breach of security of the country and regional migration issues, especially in border states of India.

To ensure that there is a secure and proper registry of the citizens of the country, the Government of India launched a scheme to issue a unique 12-digit number, termed *Aadhaar* (meaning *foundation* or *support*), to every resident of India. This lifetime unique identification can be utilized by the service providers, both in the public and private sectors, and by development organizations. The Aadhaar initiative can be considered one of India's most revolutionary and transformational technological endeavors in recent history. In little more than 6 years from its inception in 2009, there are more than 960 million people registered in Aadhaar (data as of January 2016).

This chapter explores the question of how the Aadhaar system is preparing India for analytics. The founding strategy of the Aadhaar card, its salient features, the supporting infrastructure, and some initial benefits in public service delivery are highlighted. This chapter also highlights avenues of future development by using the Aadhaar card infrastructure. The target audiences for this chapter are researchers and practitioners who seek to leverage analytics and improve social and economic health of a nation. More specifically, the opportunities that India presents for social entrepreneurs and researchers are presented in this chapter.

This chapter is divided into four sections to present to the reader various aspects of the Aadhaar initiative. The first section presents to the reader the strategic objectives behind Aadhaar and its initial communication process; the second section presents salient features of the Aadhaar infrastructure; the third section presents some public-sector initiatives that have benefited from the Aadhaar infrastructure; and the fourth section provides a road ahead by identifying avenues for further research.

Aadhaar: The Missing Link in Government Service Delivery

Strategic Objectives

Verifying the identity of citizens in India has always been a very complicated task. Several identifications were required for a person to receive public and private services. The authenticity of these documents was hard to verify, and hence, public service delivery was mostly a bad experience for the citizens. One of the first clear strategies to confirm identities initiated by the Government of India was the voter card, in 1993. This card was not well accepted by many of the 1.2 billion population, because the Election Commission had several other documents that were accepted besides the voter card to let citizens vote. Migration in border states has also been related to border security and to differentiation between citizens and migrants from across the border. In 2003, the government initiated a pilot project in the bordering states, with a focus on having a better handle on migration pattern, in turn enhancing nation's security. The project called the Multipurpose National Identity Card (MNIC) can be considered one of the main predecessors of Aadhaar. A list of documents accepted by central and state government agencies since independence (1947) and the issues related to them are presented in Table 6.1.

The Unique Identification Authority of India (UIDAI), a central government agency (http://uidai.gov.in/), was established in January 2009. The core purpose of this body was to provide unique identification to every Indian citizen. The precondition to this mandate was that the identity would be robust in nature, with a strong emphasis on elimination of duplicates and fake accounts. The mandate also required that verification of a person's identity from the registry could be done in a fast and cost-effective manner. With these key objectives in mind, the UIDAI initiated the Aadhaar card program.

Although there is no single clearly identified strategic objective of the Aadhaar card, the huge investments in this project by the Government of India clearly suggest that the program will bring several benefits to the government. First, it appears that the social programs that the Government of India has initiated for the development of people below the poverty line (BPL) have been failing to make

Table 6.1   List of National Identifications in India

IDENTITY	ISSUES	APPROX. START YEAR
National registry of citizens	Various documents' requirement and manual in nature. Often had inconsistencies.	1951
Bank/post office account	Verification process ad hoc, and numerous bogus and ghost accounts.	1947
High school/university mark sheets	Authentic to a certain extent, but lack of standards in degree certificates caused several cases of frauds.	1947
Government service card	Authentic, but this card provided support only to people employed in public service.	1947
Driving license	Could be issued from any state without much background validation. Several people had multiple driving licenses.	1947
Ration card	Was used to receive subsidies from government. Several bogus accounts, and sometimes took more than 2 years to get one.	1947
Permanent account number (PAN) card	Mostly used to track tax filings and high-value transactions. People in the BPL category do not file for tax, and hence, the vast majority of people do not have one.	1961
Voter ID card	Used as an identity to cast vote. This card is with good percentage of eligible voters (95%); however, several bogus cases have been reported.	1993

an impact. Recent reports of the World Bank have cited population in the ranges of 20%–30% (depending on the measuring criteria) to BPL. The Government of India also earmarks a sizeable percentage (nearly 60% of the social sector budget) to social development and poverty-eradication projects. The biggest challenge to public service delivery impact is its accessibility to citizens. Not having a clear list of individuals creates several issues where the remittances (funds) do not reach the targeted citizens. A flow-through problem of subsidies and funds has been well documented. The UIDAI will ensure that people in the BPL category receive the funds, and possibly, this is one of the primary strategic objectives of the Aadhaar card. It also brings people at the *bottom of the pyramid* at a level playing field with others in many ways.

Another important aspect that is a huge challenge for India is the national security. India shares land borders with several neighboring countries. Most of these neighboring countries have living indices below that of India, and this gives rise to migration toward India. India already has a population of more than 1.2 billion, and illegal immigration could add to India's worries. Besides this, national security has also been an issue, and ascertaining the identity of a person has always been a challenge for the enforcement agencies.

Communication Process

Although Aadhaar is a government-funded incentive, with significant funds invested, there is no regulation requiring mandatory use. It was hence important for the UIDAI team to emphasize the importance of this program by creating a general awareness of its benefits. Given that there are no costs incurred by the citizen in registering with Aadhaar system, the idea was that creating awareness and clearly communicating its benefits would make this program successful.

The program used several mechanisms to mobilize the masses toward registry for the Aadhaar cards. The program also identified that although Aadhaar is for every citizen of India, it would impact each strata of society differently, and hence, it was important to identify and mobilize registration in those various groups as a priority to create a high impact from the very beginning.

The Aadhaar rollout strategy is presented in Figure 6.1.

Each of the phases has several key objectives, with an underlying theory that the customer interaction should create a sense of satisfaction and belief in the Aadhaar card system.

Phase 1: Mass Awareness Phase   Before launching the Aadhaar card in any state, there is an initiative to create an awareness of the benefits of the card to the targeted citizens. Several channels are utilized to reach out to the masses, such as TV, radio, print, and digital media. The diversity of language and culture in the particular state is taken into account to ensure that the impact of such initiatives is high. This phase focuses on a rapid penetration of awareness of the program and a clear definition of the short-term benefits to the citizens. This activity usually starts approximately 30 days before actual enrollment.

Phase 2: Registration and Education   The registration process is facilitated by a group called the introducers. The primary task of the

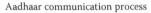

Aadhaar communication process

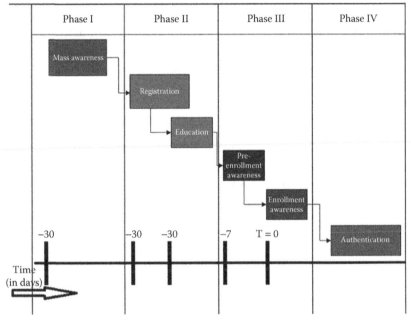

Figure 6.1 Aadhaar communication process. (UIDAI, Aadhaar—communication to a billion, an awareness and communication report, UIDAI, New Delhi, India, 2015.)

introducers is to influence the residents to get a positive buy-in. The introducers are selected in three categories:

Category 1: This category constitutes the three levels of government: federal, state, and municipal. Elected representatives from these three categories of government are mandated to influence people in their respective zones to register for the Aadhaar program.

Category 2: Non-governmental agencies (NGOs) that focus on social development of the masses and that are closely linked to the ecosystem are mandated to get people registered.

Category 3: Registrars, who actually register citizens to the Aadhaar program, and their private agencies are also given the responsibility to enroll people.

All these categories of introducers specifically educate citizens on the benefits of the Aadhaar card and walk them through the enrollment process. Another important aspect covered by the introducers, who encourage citizens to enroll to the program, is the required documentation to get the Aadhaar card. The training is conducted in such a manner that there is an organic spread of the message and benefits behind Aadhaar. These activities are usually undertaken approximately 30 days before the actual enrollment process.

Phase 3: Pre-Enrollment and During-Enrollment Awareness   The objective of the pre-enrollment awareness process is twofold: first, to refresh the message sent out during the registration process, and second, to ensure that the registration process is efficient. The message sent during the registration process is refreshed to ensure that the benefits of the Aadhaar card are clearly understood. In order to ensure that the enrollment process is smooth, it is important for the target audience to come prepared with the required documents for procurement of the Aadhaar card. This process is conducted approximately 7 days before the enrollment process.

On the day of enrollment, most of the activities undertaken by the UIDAI are operational in nature. The focus is to ensure that people attending the enrollment drive are aware of the steps for getting enrolled with the system. It is also ensured that they are trained on steps post registry, so that the efficacy of the Aadhaar card is maintained.

Phase 4: Authentication   This phase continues for the lifetime of the Aadhaar card users, where they gain benefit from having a unique identification that is verifiable in real time and in a cost-effective manner. The success of this phase is essential to generate future interest in the Aadhaar card and to ensure that the investments put into this system improve the public service delivery infrastructure.

The Aadhaar Infrastructure

In this section, we present the salient features of the Aadhaar infrastructure, highlighting how the information is gathered, stored, and accessed in the Aadhaar system. This infrastructure has taken into account the latest technologies to help ensure that the large target database of more than 1.2 billion citizens of India is secure yet accessible to validation authorities. The first subsection discusses the framework of the Aadhaar card; the second subsection highlights the technical aspects of Aadhaar infrastructure, and the third subsection highlights the authentication process.

Complete Framework of the Aadhaar

Based on the vision to create a unique national identify that could be verified in real time, the technical team of Aadhaar used certain founding principles to ensure effectiveness of the system. The key aspects taken into consideration are summarized as follows:

Open system: It was conceptualized that the Aadhaar framework should have a forward-looking design and be compatible with any technology and device in the future. The underlying Aadhaar system has a model where the native application program interfaces (APIs) can integrate with external APIs, which makes it vendor-neutral and device-independent. The data packets generated by vendor applications can be in any format, making this framework open to any technology. The Aadhaar network's open API protocol makes it easy for external organizations to integrate for validation purposes.

Load handling: The Aadhaar system is targeted toward a population of 1.2 billion people, which is continually increasing. The efficacy of the system is its ability to handle multiple transactions in a quick turnaround time. In order to facilitate this requirement of massive scalability, the Aadhaar system is supported by a load-balanced multi-location data center, using a distributed architecture, to ensure availability and quick response time. Every user generates approximately 3–5 megabytes (MB) of data, which means that this database will hold approximately 10–15 petabytes (10^{15} bytes) of data.

Data security: The storage of more than 1.2 billion identities that are biometric in nature requires a responsible approach that carefully considers security of the data. The Aadhaar card system uses state-of-the-art 2048-bit public key infrastructure (PKI) encryption. (Roughly speaking, it would take 72 million weeks to break a 56-bit encryption.) Other security vulnerabilities such as transaction data that could be used to hack into system are never stored in the Aadhaar system.

For example, when an Aadhaar cardholder goes to a bank to open an account or apply for loan, the Aadhaar system simply validates the person's identity. The transaction following the validation process is not stored in the UIDAI servers. Only biometric information and other basic details of the person that were collected during the registration process are stored in an encrypted manner in the UIDAI servers.

To ensure the availability and security of the system, the application server is designed to have different interfaces with service providers. The application server has interfaces that provide specific functions, clearly separating the enrollment and authentication systems. Within the application server, there are subservers that provide certifications to biometric service providers and their devices and open and transparent business intelligence (BI) tools for report generation. The application server is hosted as a distributed system in a private cloud with a data center infrastructure management system that ensures load balancing. A block-level view of the application server is presented in Figure 6.2.

Technical Aspects of the Aadhaar Framework

The Aadhaar system is designed with a state-of-the-art software stack to support and manage Big Data. Every care was taken to ensure that compatibility with current and future vendor systems would not be an issue. Leveraging the power of open-source capability, coupled with a database system that is equipped to handle various kinds of data, structured, semi-structured, and unstructured, the technical team of Aadhaar had to make a number of technology-related decisions. For instance, the application server resides on a Linux operating system, with most applications built in Java. The distributed storage of the data is managed by a state-of-the-art Apache Hadoop system. This technology ensures that hardware failures do not cause a bottleneck in the data save and fetch process. In order to support all formats of data and comply with the Big Data standards set forth by companies such as Facebook and Google, the database model is NoSQL. This model ensures that the rigidity of the traditional schema-based approach followed by relational database is replaced by a more flexible database system. The schema-less approach in NoSQL also facilitates a larger

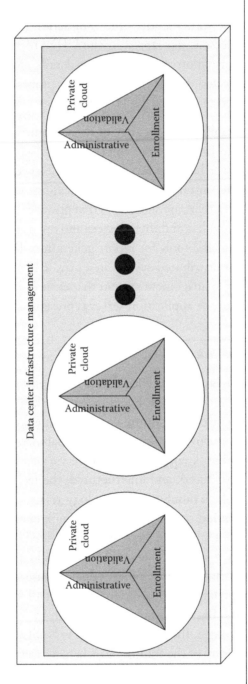

Figure 6.2 The Aadhaar infrastructure.

number of concurrent users. MangoDB, which is a growing standard supporting NoSQL, is used as a vendor for this purpose.

On the client side, the Aadhaar system uses a Windows-based system for user registration. The biometric data are sent out by several biometric devices; however, the vendors of these devices have to be registered in the central system for the enrollment system to accept the biometric data sent out during the enrollment process.

Authentication Process

The Aadhaar card carries a picture and a randomly generated unique number that stays with a person for his or her lifetime. This number is mapped to the biometric data (fingerprints and iris) and stored in an encrypted manner in the distributed secure servers managed by the UIDAI. Certain other data items are also recorded at the time of enrollment. As a mandatory requirement, the name, age, date of birth, gender, and address of the citizen are recorded. The details of the parents or guardian are recorded as conditional data. The enrollment also optionally records the phone number and email address of the person. A specimen of an Aadhaar card is presented in Figure 6.3.

The authentication process is done to validate the identity of a person. All public and private service vendors who integrate their applications with the Aadhaar system verify whether the person is actually the one who he or she claims to be. Coupled with biometric data, this validation process is far more authentic than

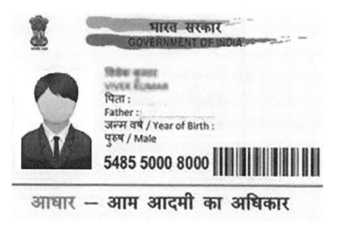

Figure 6.3   Specimen Aadhaar card. (From https://uidai.gov.in.)

many national identities such as the ones given in countries such as the United States and Canada. The sole purpose of these authentication systems is to receive a binary response (0 and 1 mapped to no and yes). This authentication process leverages the openness of the Aadhaar infrastructure and can be accessed by any service, protocol, network, or device. The only precondition is that the device sending out biometric information to the Aadhaar distributed network is a registered vendor to ensure credibility of the data and also to prevent fraudulent activities. An anti-fraud application is also present in the server, which monitors and blocks any such activities.

It is important to observe that by separation of interfaces, the Aadhaar system ensures that the data in the servers are not tampered with. The validation applications do not have the ability to make changes to the data and can only verify the identity of the person. Activities that involve Know Your Customer (KYC) for compliance have developed interfaces to identify people in real time. One such application is presented in Figure 6.4.

भारतीय स्टेट बैंक
State Bank of India

e-KYC (KNOW YOUR CUSTOMER) SERVICES
Just Three Easy Steps:

1 Provide Aadhaar Number

2 Provide Your Finger Print

3 Instant Validation with Aadhaar Database

Convenient + Faster

Figure 6.4   Aadhaar card validation process. (From http://www.sbi.co.in.)

Aadhaar: Bringing in Efficiencies in Public Service

The Government of India has outlined several initiatives to support its citizens. These initiatives reach the citizens in three delivery models. The first approach entails a direct transfer of funds to the qualifying beneficiaries, such as pensions for retired individuals and food protection money for people in the BPL category. The second approach supports subsidies such as cooking gas subsidy, which is provided to low-income houses at a lower rate. The third approach encompasses services that are provided to citizens by third-party agencies. One example of such initiative is government-funded vocational training to create a trained workforce.

All these initiatives faced some sort of mismanagement due to the lack of a proper identity-management mechanism. Several people in need would face difficulties and hardships in receiving the funds directed to them because of issues such as bogus identities and flow through losses. With an objective to increase the standard of living and to bring in equality among the citizens, the Government of India in 2014 launched the *Jan Dhan Yojna* scheme. This new scheme requires Indian families to open a bank account even with zero balance. In turn, citizens can get free life insurance for their family with this account. Within 4 months of its launch, more than 99% of the Indian households were covered under the program. The strict KYC regulations in India deter the poor and remotely located citizens from transacting with financial institutions. It can be inferred that the benefits of opening an account, coupled with the e-KYC mechanism in Aadhaar, could have been a catalyst in the massive success of this program. By now linking Aadhaar numbers to bank accounts, the Government of India can manage direct transfers and subsidies to the right individuals. Although the net impact is difficult to estimate, having a verifiable identity surely appears to have brought people closer to the government, ensuring that the leakages and corruption in the delivery system are bypassed.

India is the largest democracy in the world. The people vote for a new government every 5 years, and the voting process is managed by a body called the Election Commission of India. One of the major challenges of the commission is to ensure a fair and peaceful election.

Voter turnout is seen to be deeply correlated with the law and order situation of the nation. The last general elections had the maximum-ever turnout of more than 75% of eligible voters. The Election Commission of India is now exploring the possibility of e-voting, which can be facilitated only because of the Aadhaar card system. Several studies have been done in this direction, and hopefully, in the near future, the world's largest democracy could cast its votes by using a biometric validation system.

The Future of Aadhaar: Challenges and Avenues for Development

One of the major challenges of the Aadhaar system is the voluntary nature of this system. The Government of India is yet to pass a law that would make the Aadhaar card a mandatory requirement for every citizen. Aadhaar has also faced criticism from privacy advocates, because it collects biometric data. Even with these limitations, the UIDAI has had success in registering nearly 75% of the population (as of January 2016). It has begun to impact the lives of the poor and is slowly coming into the mainstream as the only solution for validation of the identity of Indian citizens.

Some of the privacy concerns have been addressed by the government by providing a mechanism of de-registering from the system, which will delete all biometric data that were ever stored. However, initiatives such as Digital India, where the government seeks to digitize all its business in phases, have to be catalyzed by the existence of Aadhaar card. This has given rise to several opportunities, which are supported by venture funds such as Unitus Seed Fund (http://usf.vc/) and Khosla Labs (http://www.khoslalabs.com).

We have identified three broad areas of future research and development. These areas are identified as follows:

1. Bottom-of-the-pyramid development areas
2. Counter-terrorism/law-and-order area
3. Benefits measurement mechanism

In a developing nation like India, the government spends a majority of its budget on development avenues for poverty eradication and skill development for economically weaker sections of the society. There is a big opportunity for social developmental programs, which focus on benefiting the masses. One such developmental area is disruptive payment and financial services. Companies such as Eko Financial (http://eko.co.in/) that started operations before the Aadhaar card was introduced have quickly integrated with the UIDAI validation system and have benefited in that process. One area where future developmental work would significantly impact the masses is the process of creating a credit rating system. Such systems would help the weaker sections of society to easily access credit toward their developmental initiatives. Education and skill development initiatives can be developed better if a system is developed to link Aadhaar identity with educational qualification. Using these data, the governmental and quasi-governmental agencies can initiate appropriate measures for education and vocational training. Another area of development that would significantly impact the weaker sections of the society is to develop appropriate applications that link medical records to Aadhaar. Citizens could avail subsidized benefits based on their income. Based on the financial status, a variable-cost medical service could be provided. Applications could be developed to make the citizens aware of the government and other benefits to improve their standard of living, and this could be customized and directed to every citizen.

National security is always a big concern in any country. India has been a target of various terrorist activities. Hence, it is important for the Government of India to develop counter-terrorism measures. There were some initiatives such as strict documentation to receive a mobile phone SIM card. However, due to the lack of proper validation system, several phone SIM cards were taken from bogus accounts. It has also been a challenge for enforcement agencies to keep a track of movements of known convicts. The lack of digitization of criminal records and of a proper mechanism to validate the identity of a person presents a challenge for enforcement agencies. Projects that could use the Big Data stored with the identity generated from Aadhaar could help enforcement agencies in establishing inconsistencies in the system and pave the way to a smarter enforcement system. The Aadhaar system can also be used to prevent money laundering and other black-market activities by integration of the financial systems.

Finally, the Aadhaar card is a complex project. Although this project claims to be the cheapest biometric program in the world, the utility of such a system has not been studied objectively. Several data have been presented by agencies to highlight the utility of the project, but there remains a lack of a scorecard that could highlight the impact of Aadhaar on a particular service or a business sector. Lack of enough data on the situation before the Aadhaar card was brought into picture is an impediment, but several research projects have studied the influence of such transformational projects on the macro-economic environment. Such research initiatives would provide the justification of switching to Aadhaar.

7

Visual Data Mining with Virtual Reality Spaces

Exploring Canadian Federal Government Data

JULIO J. VALDES

Contents

Introduction

The unprecedented developments in communication, sensor, and computer technologies have reshaped the world into one of constantly increasing information volumes. The so-called Internet of Things (IoT) creates a context where a plethora of objects and devices is interconnected in a network that collects and exchanges large amounts of data. Current technologies (high-throughput instruments, social networks, sensor networks, and so on) have created the information explosion and the Big Data scenarios. They require not only an information-processing counterpart but also effective mechanisms to enable human decision makers (in areas such as economics, medicine, industry, science, the military, and politics) to understand the systems from which data come and to decide on the courses of action. Increasingly, time is of the essence; therefore, mechanisms capable of speeding up the decision process are a permanent requirement.

The analysis of large masses of data, diverse in sources and in nature, becomes imperative in order to extract useful knowledge. On the one hand, it will capitalize on the investments made in developing the wide data collection and warehousing infrastructures producing the information. On the other hand, it will unfold the potential for making unforeseen discoveries in a wide variety of domains. Modern societies are now aware of the impact of data and the necessity to properly manage the data and to transform them into knowledge. However, the idea of maximizing insight into the data, uncovering the underlying structure of data, extracting important variables, detecting anomalies and oddities, and developing parsimonious models driven by the data has been pioneered and advocated for decades under the name of exploratory data analysis [1–4]. Clearly, it is with the technological advances of today that those ideas can be developed in greater extent.

The purpose of this chapter is twofold: (1) To bring to the attention of government communities working on data analytics the possibilities of a certain class of information visualization approach capable of representing large masses of highly dimensional, heterogeneous, imprecise, and incomplete data [5–7]. Large and complex bodies of information can be interactively explored with ease via simple 3D representations shaped as virtual-reality environments. This approach combines man and machine in a way that integrates the best of both, in particular, the extraordinary and fast geometric and pattern recognition capabilities of the human brain. (2) To illustrate how visual data mining and knowledge discovery processes can be performed with this kind of representations, using two real-world examples from opinion polls about Canadian Federal Government policies, with respect to a variety of topics (support and approval). Delving deeper into these processes using the techniques presented will not be covered in this chapter.

The chapter is organized as follows: Section *Information Visualization and Visual Data Mining* presents information visualization and visual data mining in the context of Big Data and the IoT, with a focus on the much-less-discussed topic of the *nature* of the information produced. Section *Virtual Reality Spaces for Information Visualization* presents approaches based on dimensionality reduction and the creation of representation spaces suitable for visual inspection of the data, based on nonlinear transformations of the original information into lower dimensional spaces. Section *Two Examples of Canadian Federal Government Data* presents two examples of publicly available Canadian Federal Government data derived from opinion polls that will be used for illustrating the application of the visualization techniques of the section *Virtual Reality Spaces for Information Visualization*. The data derived from one of the polls are of a less conventional type and cannot be processed using most of the software packages currently used by the data analytics and machine-learning communities. Section *Support for Federal Government Spending 1987–2010* presents visualization spaces constructed with the data from the section *Two Examples of Canadian Federal Government Data* and some results emerging from their visual exploration. Finally, the section *Conclusions* presents the conclusions.

Information Visualization and Visual Data Mining

In the Big Data and the IoT scenarios, information visualization stands out as a way to speed up and understand its contents [8]. Graphical mechanisms have been developed to access large data repositories and to display structural information, different kinds of relations, and queries [9]. Visual representations also aim at the meaning of information (semantics), which contrasts to scientific visualization. Information visualization typically involves dealing with non-numeric, non-spatial, and high-dimensional data [10]. However, an important and usually ignored fact is that the data produced by the information explosion are not only huge in volume but also highly heterogeneous in nature, involving numeric and non-numeric quantities, with different degrees of uncertainties, vagueness and incompleteness. The data are composed of scalar values mixed with images, signals, videos, documents, and other types of variables. In addition, the information may contain time and/or spatial dependencies. In other words, in addition to the classical types of scales recognized in statistics (nominal, ordinal, interval, and ratio), there are others, and the whole body of information can be structured and/or unstructured. From a practical point of view, it must be recalled that all data acquisition systems are fallible; therefore, missing information is inevitable. This added level of complexity to the already-existing heterogeneity and imprecision associated with the data requires the development of information processing systems that are able to work with this kind of data. They must include new paradigms, algorithms, and the computational infrastructure required to face such challenges. The use of virtual reality (VR) as an effective approach for visualizing large, high-dimensional, heterogeneous, imprecise, and incomplete data was developed in References 5–7.

In the medical domain, a typical example is the clinical record of a patient in a hospital. It contains collections of properties of very different types, like (1) non-numeric variables such as gender and pain level, (2) numeric (scalar) magnitudes such as temperature and pressure (3) more complex data such as image information (e.g., X-rays and computed tomographic [CT] scans), (4) signal data (e.g., cardiac electrocardiograms [EKG] and brain electroencephalograms [EEG]), and (5) documents containing laboratory reports, doctors' assessments of the patient, etc. In addition, the information changes with time and space (geographical location). Currently, clinical data from a patient are processed separately from the images, the signals, and other pieces of information describing the state of the patient. Images, in turn, are analyzed individually. For example, nuclear magnetic resonance images are interpreted by using applications typically provided by the equipment manufacturer, which do not incorporate other sources of information (e.g., the behavior of the heart's EKG or other variables). It is well known that in real-world systems, there is a complex interplay between the variables describing the process; however, that knowledge is lost if data processing techniques are incapable of accepting the heterogeneous nature of the information and treating the information associated with a given object as a whole, accounting for the interplay of its descriptor variables.

An example of a data table containing heterogeneous information is shown in Figure 7.1. In order to emphasize the nature of the descriptor variables, column labels indicate the type of information associated to the attribute, not the attribute name. Imprecision and vagueness are mathematically representable as fuzzy sets [11], rough sets [12], Dempster-Shafer theory [13,14], shadow sets [15], and other approaches (in Figure 7.1, triangular and trapezoidal fuzzy numbers were used). Naturally, in a real-world case, several attributes of the same type as well as attributes representing other types of information are possible. When considering large data sets,

Nominal	Ordinal	Ratio	Fuzzy	Image	Signal	Graph	Doc ...
red	small	2.5					
green	?	3.8					
blue	Big	−7.4					

Figure 7.1 Simple example of heterogeneous data in a medical context representing an objects–attributes table. Rows are patients, and columns are attributes (variables). "?" indicates that the attribute value is missing.

the usual consideration is about the number of objects, individuals, observation, or samples, which nowadays is in the order of hundreds of thousands or millions. However, there is another, less emphasized aspect, that is, the number of descriptor variables or attributes characterizing those objects, which may scale up to be hundreds and tens of thousands. For example, in medicine, biopsies for genetic studies are often described by the expression activity of tens of thousands of genes. When other properties of the biopsies are incorporated, such as cell images and other laboratory measurements, the information becomes not only highly multidimensional but also heterogeneous.

Information visualization is seen as the study of how to effectively present information via graphical approaches, with the purpose of assisting cognitive and problem-solving processes. In general, it goes beyond the mere use of eyesight to include a broader variety of sensory representations. Most techniques rely on 2D or 3D color graphics, either static or interactive, with or without some forms of animation, with the purpose of allowing the user to explore and navigate through the specific information represented. Ultimately, the goal is to exploit the built-in capabilities of the brain and the senses, to effectively and quickly process information obtained and stored in ways not amenable to direct human consumption. By means of the senses, particularly sight, hearing, and touch, humans can incorporate large amounts of information, with the brain representing the data-processing counterpart. The brain is an extraordinary complex system with a low-power, massively parallel processing capability, which transforms and synthesizes raw information into abstract constructs.

Although the so-called scientific visualization involves data with an inherent physical component [16], such as the ones typically coming from research on natural sciences or engineering, abstract data visualization involves information that has no inherent mapping to a physical space [17]. Common examples are object-attribute databases, opinion polls, and preference rankings, just to mention a few. They pose numerous challenges, and this is the type of information that is explored in this paper.

Virtual Reality Spaces for Information Visualization

The analysis of high-dimensional data such as the ones produced by the information explosion is a complex problem. As seen in the section *Information Visualization and Visual Data Mining*, data sets are large not only from the point of view of the number of observations contained within but also from the point of view of the number of descriptor variables. In the particular case where all of them are scalar, real-valued, that number is the dimensionality of the original space. Geometrically, every object (e.g., observation) can be seen as a point in a space of a dimension given by the number of descriptor variables. Nowadays, original data spaces involving many thousands of variables (i.e., highly multidimensional) are commonplace. Typically, the observations come from real-world physical systems, where their variables are interrelated in complex ways and contain noise, redundancies, distortions introduced by instruments or data acquisition procedures, artifacts, and other issues. In such circumstances, the amount of useful information is not proportional to the cardinality of the set of descriptor variables.

Humans perceive most of the information through vision, in large quantities and at very high input rates. The human brain is extremely well qualified for the fast understanding of complex geometries and visual patterns and still outperforms computers. Virtual reality is an appropriate paradigm for information representation. In the first place, to interact with a virtual scene, minimal skills are required [18]. Other notable properties of VR are as follows: (1) it is flexible (it allows the choice of different representation models to better suit human perception preferences); (2) it allows immersion (the user can navigate inside the data and interact with the objects in the world); (3) it creates a living experience (the user is not merely a passive observer but an actor in the world); and (4) VR is broad and deep (the user may see the VR world as a whole and/or concentrate on specific details of the world) [19].

Intrinsic Dimension

In high-dimensional spaces, the volumes of neighborhoods of a fixed size become large very quickly with the increase in dimension. This poses a problem when constructing reliable estimates of probability density distributions, because the number of points required grows exponentially (the *curse of dimensionality* [20]). In addition to data sparsity, real-world data spaces are not filled uniformly. Points are often concentrated in lower-dimension subspaces of complex shapes, which are embedded within the higher-dimensional one. The dimension of these subspaces or manifolds is found to be of much lower dimensionality than the original data representation spaces. It means that, in fact, the data are not really of high dimension. The performance of data analytic and machine-learning procedures degrades considerably with the increase in the number of dimensions to the extent that it is considered that data analytic methods work when applied to high-dimensional data just because, in reality, the data are not of high dimension. The notion of intrinsic dimension (ID) emerges (informally) as the number of parameters (or degrees of freedom) required to describe all of the data [21]. A simple but frequently inadequate estimator is the number of eigenvalues required to reach 97.5% of the cumulated variance (EigValue). Other principles used in algorithms are maximum likelihood (MLE) [22], correlation dimension (CorrDim) [23], the geodesic minimal spanning tree (GMST) [24], and so on.

A distinction must be made between the ID of a data set and the dimension of the space used for constructing its visual representation. While the former depends on the internal structure of the data, the latter is ultimately chosen by the user and is constrained by the human perception system (1D to 3D). Evidently, when both are close, a visual representation of (an approximation of) the subspace, with dimension equal to ID, would provide an object where a reliable interpretation of the internal structure of the data can be made.

Nonlinear Transformations and Manifold Learning

Once the dimension of the target space is decided upon, the next step is to construct the space representing the original information. Learning these subspaces or data manifolds is important and useful for understanding the internal structure of the data and for improving the performance of data analytics methods such as clustering, classification, and regression. However, depending on the complexity of the information, dimensionality reduction is usually a difficult task, and different approaches have been proposed for learning the subspace.

The representation of distance matrices in low-dimensional spaces, including dissimilarities, has been studied within multidimensional scaling [25–27]. These techniques seek distance/dissimilarity preservation between an original low-dimensional space and a target low-dimensional space. When successful, objects that are close/far from each other in the original space should appear close/far in the low-dimensional space. The idea is that dissimilarities δ_{ij} in the original space are represented geometrically as distances d_{ij} in the target space, weighted in different ways. Mathematically, this notion is expressed as a cost, error, or information loss function that becomes an objective of a minimization process that provides a set of low-dimensional vectors. Different methods have been proposed along the lines of this general formulation. Among them, Sammon's nonlinear mapping [28] has been extensively used. It considers the transformation of vectors of two spaces of different dimension ($D > m$) as given by the mapping $\varphi : \mathbb{R}^D \to \mathbb{R}^m$, which maps vectors $\vec{x} \in \mathbb{R}^D$ to vectors $\vec{y} \in \mathbb{R}^m, \vec{y} = \varphi(\vec{x})$.

$$\text{Sammon error} = \frac{1}{\sum\limits_{i<j} \delta_{ij}} \sum\limits_{i<j} \frac{(\delta_{ij} - d(\vec{y}_i, \vec{y}_j))^2}{\delta_{ij}} \quad (7.1)$$

where d is a distance in $\mathbb{R}^m$ (Euclidean is the usual choice). The weight term δ_{ij}^{-1} gives more importance to the preservation of smaller distances rather than larger ones and is determined by the dissimilarity distribution in the data space. Typically, Equation 7.1 is solved with classical numeric optimization techniques [29], starting with an initial approximation that is refined in successive iterations until a convergence criterion is met. Accordingly, φ exists as an implicit function. When constructing a VR space for visualization, it is convenient to use a mapping function given by the composition:

$$\Phi = (\Psi \circ \varphi)(\vec{x}) \tag{7.2}$$

where Ψ is a linear principal component transformation (in the low-dimensional nonlinear space) and $\vec{x}$ is an object in the original, higher-dimensional space [30]. In this way, the nonlinear axes are oriented in the direction of the maximal monotonically decreasing variance, which helps in the interpretation.

Another technique for constructing low-dimensional spaces for data representation is the t-Distributed Stochastic Neighbor Embedding (t-SNE) [31]. It is an improved variant of the non-linear dimensionality reduction technique, Stochastic Neighbor Embedding (SNE) [32], with better properties. The latter starts by converting the high-dimensional Euclidean distances between objects into conditional probabilities that represent similarities. The similarity of objects x_j to objects x_i is the conditional probability that x_i would pick x_j as its neighbor if neighbors were picked in proportion to their probability density under a Gaussian distribution centered at x_i. A corresponding similarity measure is defined for the low-dimensional counterparts of the points, and the SNE minimizes the sum of Kullback–Leibler divergences over all objects for the two conditional probability distributions.

$$C = \sum_i \sum_j p_{ij} \log \frac{p_{ij}}{q_{ij}}$$

where p_{ij} is the conditional probability of point j to be the neighbor of point i in the original space, and q_{ij} is its lower-dimensional space counterpart.

This method depends on a parameter called perplexity, which can be interpreted as a smooth measure of the effective number of neighbors (related to the entropy of the distribution, in turn controlled by its variance and the procedure searches for the variance required for producing a user-specified perplexity). The t-SNE has the following two advantages on SNE: (1) it uses a symmetrized version of the SNE objective function with simpler gradients, and (2) it uses a Student-t distribution rather than a Gaussian distribution to compute the similarity between two points in the low-dimensional space. A heavy-tailed distribution in the low-dimensional space alleviates optimization problems of SNE and the disparity of the areas where distant and nearby points should be accommodated. The t-SNE is capable of capturing much of the local structure of the high-dimensional data very well, while also revealing global structure such as the presence of clusters at several scales.

It is important to note that both mapping techniques are *unsupervised*. That is, the learning process is guided by no other information than the one provided by the descriptor variables (there is no class or target variable).

Regardless of the particular technique chosen for constructing the low-dimensional space representing the data, the images of the original objects in that space, plus other relationships existing in the data (classes, hierarchies, time dependencies, etc.), are shaped as a VR scene in an appropriate 3D language (Vrml, X3D, etc.) [5–7]. The scene can be rendered with a broad variety of hardware systems, ranging from a cell phone or a laptop to a dedicated environment such as a cave. In them, the user can navigate and interact with the information in a variety of ways, ultimately entering into an exploration process that now relies on the user's built-in perception capabilities and not on his knowledge of the mathematical complexities associated with the construction of the scene. Such a machine–man approach speeds up the process of interpretation, data understanding, and knowledge discovery and has been successfully applied to several real-world domains [19,33,34].

Two Examples of Canadian Federal Government Data

In order to illustrate the visualization techniques presented in the previous section and their potential in the analysis of government information in general, data from the Canadian Opinion Research Archive at Queen's University are used [35]. This open service makes available commercial and independent surveys to academic, research, and journalistic communities. It was founded in 1992, and it contains hundreds of surveys, including thousands of discrete items collected by major commercial Canadian firms, dating back to the 1970s. In particular, two data sets were constructed by integrating information coming from Canadian opinion poll results on different topics over time [36]. Considering that the information is constantly being updated as data are added to the archive, a snapshot of two of the several specific topics available was made in October 2016. The chosen ones were support for federal Government Spending and Federal Government Approval. They were purposely chosen for several reasons: (1) even though the number of descriptor variables cannot be considered very highly dimensional on any of the data sets, it is large enough as to make it difficult, if not impossible, to reveal the underlying structure by inspection, despite of the small number of objects; (2) both sets are small from the point of view of the number of objects, which makes easier the comparison of the patterns exhibited by the visualization with the actual data; (3) in the case of the federal approval data, the type of the descriptor variables is not scalar, thus making it impossible to process the data set with most conventional statistical or machine-learning packages; (4) both data sets address interesting questions related to the way in which citizens perceive and evaluate government policies from a set of indicators, not individually, but as a whole, thus providing a more holistic perspective; and (5) they illustrate to government officials, analysts, and policy makers the possibilities of advanced information visualization procedures in providing insights, knowledge discoveries, and data understanding, quickly and effectively.

Support for Federal Government Spending 1987–2010

This survey was oriented to obtain information about how Canadian citizens support Federal Government Spending policies, with respect to the following 20 aspects: assistance to poorer regions, child care, creating jobs, defense, education, energy development, environmental protection, support for farmers, justice system, arts and culture, health care, housing, services for the elderly, services for the poor, technology research, transportation services, welfare, employment insurance, aboriginal peoples, and reducing child poverty.

The information was obtained by formulating to the subject a specific question addressing each topic. For example, in the case of *assistance to poorer regions* it was *Keeping in mind that increasing services could increase taxes, do you think the federal government is spending too much, just the right amount, or should be spending more on each of the following: programs to help the economy in poorer regions?* This question was reformulated from 2003 onward, but it kept the same meaning. A similar situation happened with the questions addressing some of the aforementioned topics.

Because not all of the topics were covered in all of the years between 1987 and 2010, a subset of them (9) was chosen: assistance to poorer regions, child care, creating jobs, education, support for farmers, health care, services for the elderly, services for the poor, and transportation services. In this way, the selected data covers information about a reasonable number of years (20 in between 1987 and 2010). Considering that each topic involves information about whether the spending is judged by the subject as {too much, just right, should be more}, the total number of descriptor variables is 27. The data set, containing 20 individuals (years) and 27 attributes (topics), is presented in Table 7.1. In order to put the opinion poll data in context, the political party in power for each year was incorporated into the table as an additional, last variable.

Federal Government Approval 1990–2009

This survey was oriented to obtain information about how Canadian citizens approve federal government policies with respect to the following 11 aspects: aboriginal and native issues, defense, deficit reduction, economy, environment, federal–provincial relations, foreign policy, health care, taxation, unemployment, Canada–U.S. relations. The information was obtained by formulating a specific question to the subject addressing each topic. For example, in the case of *aboriginal and native issues*, it was "*Generally speaking, do you approve or disapprove of the way the current federal government is handling Aboriginal and native issues?*" (http://www.queensu.ca/cora/_trends/Ap_Aboriginal.htm). During 1990–2009, surveys addressing these topics were conducted, and sometimes, more than

Table 7.1 Support for Federal Government Spending from 1987 to 2010 (in Percentage of the Interviewed Subjects/Year Supporting a Given Spending Category)

YEAR	ASSISTANCE TO POORER REGIONS			CHILD CARE			CREATING JOBS		
	TOO MUCH	JUST RIGHT	SPEND MORE	TOO MUCH	JUST RIGHT	SPEND MORE	TOO MUCH	JUST RIGHT	SPEND MORE
1987	6.4	27.5	57.2	14.2	32.3	42.6	9.1	21.0	66.0
1988	5.4	28.5	58.4	16.5	37.0	39.7	8.1	28.5	59.6
1989	9.1	29.4	55.5	15.0	27.0	52.2	11.0	25.5	59.2
1990	6.1	26.6	60.9	13.5	34.7	46.3	10.8	22.5	62.5
1991	8.7	31.0	53.1	19.8	34.2	37.2	10.9	20.3	63.7
1992	7.2	29.3	57.1	15.1	36.9	41.0	7.1	18.5	71.4
1993	10.0	32.0	50.3	17.4	33.7	42.1	8.3	19.3	68.4
1994	12.0	32.9	48.0	16.1	35.7	42.0	12.4	25.2	58.4
1995	12.3	34.6	45.0	15.6	35.2	42.1	12.7	21.7	60.5
1996	8.4	32.9	49.0	11.6	35.8	42.2	10.4	21.8	62.7
1997	9.3	31.8	51.4	13.0	36.0	41.5	9.8	21.1	64.5
1998	7.9	32.7	51.3	10.3	35.6	45.7	9.1	22.6	63.4
1999	6.6	33.3	52.7	10.4	33.4	49.0	8.5	26.7	60.9
2003	8.8	29.8	59.9	10.3	34.4	53.3	12.8	30.0	55.6
2004	6.2	27.0	66.1	10.0	34.4	55.0	10.9	33.4	54.7
2005	6.4	27.4	65.3	14.0	33.6	51.6	11.7	32.8	54.7
2006	6.0	26.0	67.2	10.3	29.1	59.7	9.4	26.7	63.1
2007	7.8	30.2	60.0	12.4	34.5	51.5	13.1	37.6	48.0
2008	4.9	28.9	64.3	8.2	28.8	61.5	5.0	27.2	66.9
2010	7.5	30.8	58.9	10.9	37.2	49.1	10.8	30.3	57.0
YEAR	EDUCATION			SUPPORT FOR FARMERS			HEATH CARE		
	TOO MUCH	JUST RIGHT	SPEND MORE	TOO MUCH	JUST RIGHT	SPEND MORE	TOO MUCH	JUST RIGHT	SPEND MORE
1987	5.9	44.0	46.6	8.2	32.8	48.2	3.4	58.9	35.1
1988	4.1	42.9	49.4	7.9	36.9	48.5	3.0	48.8	46.5
1989	4.5	34.4	58.7	13.1	39.7	37.1	3.3	42.3	52.8
1990	3.6	40.7	53.8	9.6	35.3	48.3	3.7	57.5	36.9
1991	4.8	38.5	53.5	11.5	33.4	45.1	4.7	52.6	40.2
1992	5.2	34.8	57.5	13.6	39.4	38.4	6.6	53.9	37.5
1993	83.0	36.0	53.3	15.5	43.9	31.1	9.1	49.9	39.2
1994	7.1	33.3	57.1	18.6	43.4	28.1	7.0	48.8	42.3
1995	6.9	34.5	55.1	17.7	43.1	26.5	6.9	41.4	49.1
1996	5.2	32.4	58.6	12.0	43.5	26.7	3.8	33.4	60.4

(*Continued*)

Table 7.1 (*Continued*) Support for Federal Government Spending from 1987 to 2010 (in Percentage of the Interviewed Subjects/Year Supporting a Given Spending Category)

	EDUCATION			SUPPORT FOR FARMERS			HEATH CARE		
YEAR	TOO MUCH	JUST RIGHT	SPEND MORE	TOO MUCH	JUST RIGHT	SPEND MORE	TOO MUCH	JUST RIGHT	SPEND MORE
1997	4.7	27.5	64.2	11.1	44.2	32.6	2.2	26.4	69.5
1998	3.8	26.2	67.3	8.8	46.4	32.2	2.4	19.0	76.0
1999	2.4	24.3	71.2	8.7	38.3	43.6	2.3	21.3	75.4
2003	3.6	23.0	72.3	10.7	38	48.4	2.8	17.1	79.6
2004	3.0	22.8	73.9	9.1	38.6	51.5	3.7	18.9	77.0
2005	2.2	17.2	80.0	7.9	37.7	53.1	2.7	15.4	81.2
2006	1.9	19.5	78.2	9.7	37.3	51.2	2.0	16.9	80.5
2007	3.0	25.6	70.0	11.0	41.6	45.3	3.8	15.9	79.3
2008	1.5	21.8	75.2	8.7	39.1	49.8	2.9	18.2	78.5
2010	3.8	26.2	69.1	9.7	38.5	48.8	3.9	26.1	69.6

	SERVICES FOR THE ELDERLY			SERVICES FOR THE POOR			TRANSPORTATION SERVICES		
YEAR	TOO MUCH	JUST RIGHT	SPEND MORE	TOO MUCH	JUST RIGHT	SPEND MORE	TOO MUCH	JUST RIGHT	SPEND MORE
1987	2.1	34.5	60.2	7.6	37.2	49.3	10.0	64.3	17.1
1988	2.5	37.0	57.2	5.8	35.2	54.1	8.7	64.4	19.4
1989	2.1	31.6	63.1	7.9	32.8	54.6	13.1	56.0	24.6
1990	2.6	38.1	56.3	6.7	35.1	53.6	8.8	60.2	25.3
1991	3.0	41.4	51.2	9.4	37.6	48.1	12.7	58.6	21.5
1992	3.4	42.0	50.6	10.3	36.2	49.1	14.3	61.7	16.9
1993	4.8	47.7	43.9	12.8	39.2	43.0	14.2	62.7	16.0
1994	4.7	43.4	48.0	12.7	41.0	42.4	16.8	59.3	16.5
1995	5.2	42.6	47.8	11.7	41.1	41.6	16.9	58.8	14.9
1996	3.6	37.9	53.6	10.0	38.2	45.7	11.2	61.0	17.8
1997	2.5	35.6	56.8	9.4	35.5	50.9	12.3	56.3	21.3
1998	2.6	33.7	58.2	7.0	36.5	50.3	10.7	58.2	21.7
1999	2.7	33.4	60.2	5.5	36.5	53.0	9.7	59.2	23.1
2003	3.8	31.4	63.7	8.0	36.4	54.5	8.5	36.5	54.1
2004	2.9	30.9	65.6	7.6	32.4	59.2	6.4	36.1	57.0
2005	2.5	30.6	66.1	7.2	30.9	61.5	6.5	31.5	61.6
2006	3.4	26.7	69.1	5.6	27.3	65.5	5.1	34.3	59.8
2007	3.5	25.7	70.0	7.8	29.8	60.4	6.8	32.9	58.9
2008	1.8	27.9	69.8	6.4	31.6	60.4	3.6	35.1	60.5
2010	3.4	25.4	70.5	9.2	33.6	54.9	7.7	36.8	53.6

(*Continued*)

Table 7.1 (*Continued*)   Support for Federal Government Spending from 1987 to 2010 (in Percentage of the Interviewed Subjects/Year Supporting a Given Spending Category)

YEAR	PARTY IN GOVERNMENT
1987	Conservative
1988	Conservative
1989	Conservative
1990	Conservative
1991	Conservative
1992	Conservative
1993	Conservative
1994	Liberal
1995	Liberal
1996	Liberal
1997	Liberal
1998	Liberal
1999	Liberal
2003	Liberal
2004	Liberal
2005	Liberal
2006	Conservative
2007	Conservative
2008	Conservative
2010	Conservative

Source: Canadian Opinion Research Archive at Queen's University. Trends. http://www.queensu.ca/cora/3trends.html (with the political parties as additional information).

one survey was conducted within the same year. Not surprisingly, they exhibit changes of opinion. In order to have a closer insight and to explore the variation of the subjects' opinions, the information about each topic was aggregated into the minimum and maximum percentages of approval for each topic for each year. Therefore, for each year, the value for the approval associated with each topic is an interval of percentages, rather than a scalar value (as it would be if, e.g., the mean had been used). The interval data is somewhat more complex but richer in information. Table 7.2 presents the information about 13 years and their corresponding approval percentage intervals.

Table 7.2   Aggregated Data with the Minimum and Maximum Percentages of Approval for Different Policies of the Canadian Federal Government

YEAR	ABORIGINAL AND NATIVE ISSUES [MINIMUM, MAXIMUM]	DEFENSE [MINIMUM, MAXIMUM]	DEFICIT REDUCTION [MINIMUM, MAXIMUM]	ECONOMY [MINIMUM, MAXIMUM]	ENVIRONMENT [MINIMUM, MAXIMUM]	FEDERAL PROVINCIAL RELATIONS [MINIMUM, MAXIMUM]
1990	[16.6, 16.6]	[40.6, 42.5]	[15.2, 18.4]	[14.9, 22.5]	[29.0, 37.0]	[19.4, 26.3]
1991	[15.5, 22.1]	[40.0, 47.6]	[11.2, 16.6]	[10.2, 14.8]	[34.4, 39.3]	[18.7, 24.4]
1992	[21.2, 30.9]	[41.6, 46.5]	[7.3, 13.8]	[6.9, 13.3]	[40.4, 48.5]	[18.2, 27.4]
1993	[21.8, 24.1]	[40.0, 44.2]	[9.9, 18.1]	[10.9, 24.3]	[43.9, 48.4]	[22.4, 33.0]
1994	[25.2, 26.8]	[44.4, 48.3]	[16.7, 23.2]	[29.3, 33.0]	[49.7, 54.8]	[34.3, 37.1]
1995	[19.0, 24.1]	[42.8, 47.7]	[19.4, 25.4]	[26.3, 30.0]	[53.9, 55.4]	[28.8, 36.9]
2003	[41.3, 43.7]	[41.0, 48.4]	[53.3, 57.3]	[56.1, 61.6]	[51.7, 60.2]	[39.5, 45.0]
2004	[35.1, 44.2]	[43.5, 49.2]	[51.7, 56.9]	[50.6, 62.3]	[44.7, 52.7]	[41.6, 64.0]
2005	[36.1, 40.7]	[47.4, 47.6]	[48.2, 55.9]	[51.3, 52.7]	[42.4, 47.0]	[42.5, 45.5]
2006	[32.3, 36.2]	[46.1, 49.0]	[44.0, 57.5]	[52.6, 61.7]	[35.0, 38.7]	[47.5, 52.6]
2007	[30.4, 46.2]	[40.5, 61.8]	[46.5, 66.2]	[56.7, 75.1]	[34.8, 42.7]	[37.6, 55.4]
2008	[30.2, 39.8]	[40.2, 45.3]	[48.4, 50.5]	[38.4, 53.9]	[34.4, 38.6]	[41.5, 50.0]
2009	[36.4, 40.3]	[50.1, 50.1]	[35.9, 45.6]	[44.4, 51.6]	[38.4, 43.0]	[44.3, 44.3]

YEAR	FOREIGN POLICY [MINIMUM, MAXIMUM]	HEALTHCARE [MINIMUM, MAXIMUM]	TAXATION [MINIMUM, MAXIMUM]	UNEMPLOYMENT [MINIMUM, MAXIMUM]	CANADA-U.S. RELATIONS [MINIMUM, MAXIMUM]
1990	[43.3, 46.8]	[61.4, 67.1]	[10.6, 14.3]	[16.8, 25.3]	[42.9, 46.4]
1991	[40.8, 42.9]	[60.8, 70.1]	[8.8, 14.0]	[11.6, 17.6]	[25.1, 39.3]
1992	[36.5, 43.3]	[57.1, 69.2]	[8.8, 9.3]	[8.2, 14.8]	[28.0, 41.1]
1993	[39.7, 41.8]	[57.5, 60.6]	[9.5, 15.4]	[10.1, 20.3]	[38.2, 50.0]
1994	[45.7, 47.2]	[50.5, 58.4]	[13.9, 17.8]	[22.3, 28.6]	[51.2, 56.2]
1995	[41.9, 48.2]	[41.1, 52.7]	[15.2, 19.2]	[18.5, 24.0]	[52.0, 59.1]
2003	[54.3, 68.0]	[32.5, 40.3]	[30.4, 40.7]	[3.6, 4.0]	[47.8, 57.5]
2004	[54.0, 60.2]	[31.8, 48.2]	[32.6, 44.0]	[3.1, 4.0]	[51.5, 56.4]
2005	[51.3, 56.1]	[32.2, 37.8]	[36.0, 43.0]	[3.8, 4.2]	[46.3, 52.2]
2006	[43.1, 47.8]	[31.5, 42.2]	[32.0, 50.4]	[2.9, 4.3]	[47.8, 54.0]

Source: Canadian Opinion Research Archive at Queen's University. Trends. http://www.queensu.ca/cora/3trends.html.

Results

Support for Federal Government Spending 1987–2010

This data set is composed of 20 objects and 27 scalar real-valued descriptor variables from Table 7.1. In a preprocessing step, all values were converted to z-scores by subtracting the mean and dividing by the standard deviation of each variable. This transformation ensures that all variables will contribute to the distances in the same way (i.e., variables are equally weighted). Other approaches could have been taken, weighting some topics more than others, according to additional knowledge or viewpoints introduced by the analyst. However, an unbiased treatment was applied.

As explained in the section *Support for Federal Government Spending 1987–2010*, an extra variable was incorporated with the information of the political party in power in the year of the data collection. This variable was not involved in any of the unsupervised processing performed with the methods described in the section *Virtual Reality Spaces for Information Visualization*, and its role was only to provide context to the patterns emerging from the visualization as an overlaid, independent information. As a first step, estimations of the intrinsic dimensionality of the data using the techniques presented in the section *Intrinsic Dimension* were obtained in order to have an idea about the way in which information is distributed through the 27D space defined by the descriptor variables. The results are shown in Table 7.3. With the exception of the EigValue approach, that is, just a 97.7% cumulated variance-based number of principal component eigenvalues (a linear mapping), all other (nonlinear) estimators suggest an approximate range in between 2.6 and 4. Accordingly, a representation of the data in a 3D space would capture practically all of the information contained in the 27 original descriptor variables, with the additional advantage that it can be visually inspected.

Spaces obtained with the two mapping techniques described in the section *Nonlinear Transformations and Manifold Learning* were computed. For both Sammon's mapping and t-SNE, Euclidean distances were used when finding implicit solutions via numeric methods.

Table 7.3 Federal Government Spending (1987–2010). Intrinsic Dimensionality Estimations

METHOD	INTRINSIC DIMENSION
EigValue	5
MLE	3.993281
CorrDim	2.653355
GMST	3.210188

Clearly, it is impossible to show interactive VR environments on hard media. Accordingly, only snapshots of the 3D models can be presented, which, in addition, experience unavoidable distortions when projected to the 2D space of a page. A snapshot of the 3D representation of the federal Government Spending data set obtained with Equation 7.2 (where φ is Sammon's mapping), is shown in Figure 7.2. Every sphere represents the 3D image of a 27D vector corresponding to a row in Table 7.1, with labels indicating the year when the information was obtained. The distance between any two of them in Figure 7.2 is an indication of how similar or different the opinions for the given years are, with respect to *all* of the indicators considered in the 1987–2010 polls. This is the result of solving Equation 7.2 (which implies minimizing Equation 7.1, where δ_{ij} are the distances in the original 27D space and $d(\bar{y}_i, \bar{y}_j)$ are the corresponding ones in the transformed 3D space). In other words, the geometric location of the information corresponding to each year indicates the similarity relation between the opinions from the point of view of the questions posed in the polls. Overlaid is the information about which political party was in power. It is represented with white and black colors, which were chosen at random: years where the Conservative Party was in power are colored in white, whereas those where the Liberal Party was in power are colored in black. It is important to note that this information was

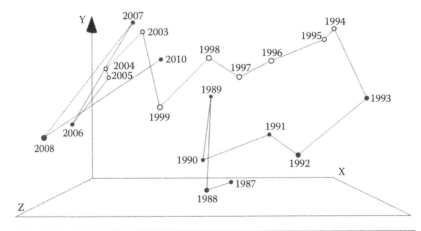

Figure 7.2   Federal Government Spending data (1987–2010): Virtual reality space with Sammon's mapping of the original data. Line segments join subsequent years. Colors indicate the political party in power during the given year: white = Liberal, black = Conservative (colors were chosen at random).

added *a posteriori* and was not used in the computation of the visualization space (*unsupervised*). Therefore, the geometric patterns emerging from the solution of Equation 7.2 were conditioned by the properties of the descriptor variables. Any relationship found between these patterns and any other external variable is due to the existence of interdependencies between that variable and the original descriptors.

The two most different opinions about government spending are those expressed in the years 1993 and 2008, both about Conservative policies (the two most distant objects in Figure 7.2). The bar chart of Figure 7.3 presents a decomposition of the elements contributing to the observed Euclidean distance between 1993 and 2008. For each of the questions in the poll, the signed squared difference between the responses is shown. The sign is determined by the difference between the response to a given question in 1993 and the corresponding one in 2008, and it indicates the direction of the individual change (larger or smaller percentages). The squared differences were normalized by their maximum, so that those with absolute values larger than 0.5 are the ones more contributing to the observed distance. Accordingly, child care, education, health care, services for the elderly, services for the poor, and transportation were the topics mostly associated with the major change of opinion between the two years.

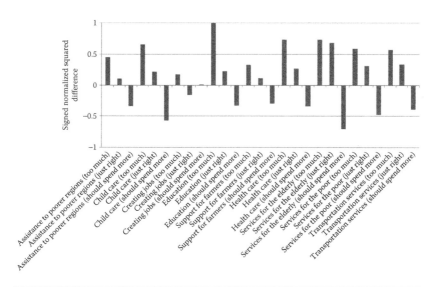

Figure 7.3   Federal Government Spending (1987–2010): Signed squared differences between the opinions expressed for years 1993 and 2008 for the topics covered by the polls.

Another interesting feature from Figure 7.2 is the clear differentiation of the distribution of the opinions between the two Conservative Party government periods 1987–1993 and 2006–2010. It means that citizens feel about the spending policies applied between the two periods in a very different way. For the Liberal Party, only one government period is covered by the 1994–2005 time range of the data. Interestingly, at the beginning of their period in power (1994), citizens' opinion started to differentiate from those expressed at the end of the first Conservative time (1993) (though not too drastically). However, as time went by, the opinions about their policies progressively changed to judgments emitted during the second phase of Conservative government. In the case of Liberal spending policies, people's opinion experienced a steady migration between the two extremes, expressed as a clearly defined trend.

Several major trends can be identified in Figure 7.2, which are shown in Figure 7.4 for clarity: (1) one trend starts at the initial years of the first Conservative government (1987–1990 to 1993), which shows a steady drift, particularly between 1990 and 1993; (2) another trend is the one described earlier, characterizing the Liberal period, which also exhibits continuous (longer) drift, but that represents a drastic reversal with respect to (1); and (3) a succession of four different short-term swings of opinion, all occurring during the second

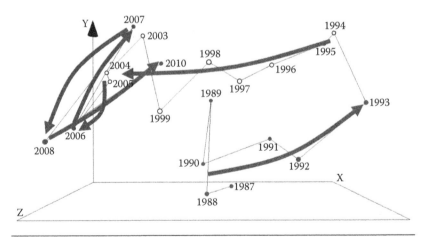

Figure 7.4   Federal Government Spending data (1987–2010): Virtual reality space with Sammon's mapping of the original data. Line segments join subsequent years. Colors indicate the political party in power during the given year: white = Liberal, black = Conservative (colors were chosen at random). Arrows indicate major opinion change trends.

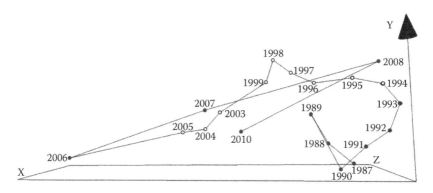

Figure 7.5 Federal Government Spending policies (1987–2010): Virtual reality space with t-SNE mapping. Line segments join subsequent years. Colors indicate the political party in power during the given year: white = Liberal, black = Conservative (colors were chosen at random).

period of the Conservative Party and exhibiting abrupt changes in direction. Opinions come close and far from those expressed about years with Liberal government in short periods of time. In comparison, the two Conservative periods in power behaved very differently from the point of view of how their spending policies were perceived.

The visualization space constructed using the t-SNE method from the section *Nonlinear Transformations and Manifold Learning* is shown in Figure 7.5. It is important to note that the small size of the data affects the quality of the space obtained with this technique, because it operates with probabilities whose estimation will be much less accurate. In addition, point neighborhoods will be defined by too little number of elements. However, the t-SNE space exhibits most of the features present in the one from Figure 7.2, with the exception of some of the events characterizing the second Conservative period. The major opinion-change trends, shown in Figure 7.6, are similar to those identified in Figure 7.4, including most of the reversals.

Federal Government Approval 1990–2009

In the case of Table 7.2, there are 13 objects and 11 attributes. However, they are interval-valued, rather than scalar, real-valued quantities. In the spirit of processing heterogeneous information (the section *Information Visualization and Visual Data Mining*), the computation of visualization spaces using the techniques described in the section *Nonlinear Transformations and Manifold Learning* requires the

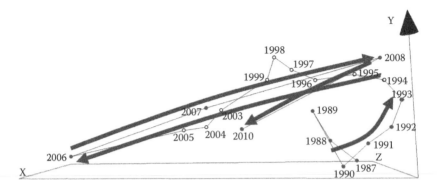

Figure 7.6   Federal Government Spending policies (1987–2010): Virtual reality space with t-SNE mapping. Line segments join subsequent years. Colors indicate the political party in power during the given year: white = Liberal, black = Conservative (colors were chosen at random). Arrows indicate major opinion change trends.

specification of a suitable dissimilarity criterion to operate with the objects in the original space of the descriptor variables.

The similarity between numeric intervals introduced in this paper conceptually combines set-theoretical concepts with geometric intuition. It is defined as a convex combination of a set similarity term and a centroid similarity (via Euclidean distances). If $A = [a_1, a_2]$ and $B = [b_1, b_2]$ are two numeric intervals with $a_1, a_2, b_1, b_2 \in \mathbb{R}$, two similarity indices (S_d^I and S_e^I) are defined as:

$$S_d^I(A,B) = \alpha * \left(\frac{A \cap B}{A \cup B} \right) + (1-\alpha) * \left(\frac{1}{1+d} \right)$$

$$S_e^I(A,B) = \alpha * \left(\frac{A \cap B}{A \cup B} \right) + (1-\alpha) * \left(\exp^{(-k*d)} \right)$$

(7.3)

where $\cap$ and $\cup$ are the intersection and union, respectively; when the intervals are treated as sets, $d = |\, mean(A) - mean(B)\,|$, $k \in \mathbb{R}^+$ and $\alpha \in [0,1]$. In general, $S_d^I, S_e^I \in [0,1]$, but when $\alpha = 1$, they are in $[0,1]$. Both measures represent a trade-off between interval overlapping and overall separation. In this chapter, the simpler S_d^I similarity index was used, with $\alpha = 0.5$ (an equal treatment of overlapping and separation). In order to obtain a 3D mapping using Equations 7.2 and 7.1, δ_{ij} was set to $((1/S_d^I(i,j)) - 1)$.

Using the same conventions of the section *Support for Federal Government Spending 1987–2010*, the VR space obtained is shown

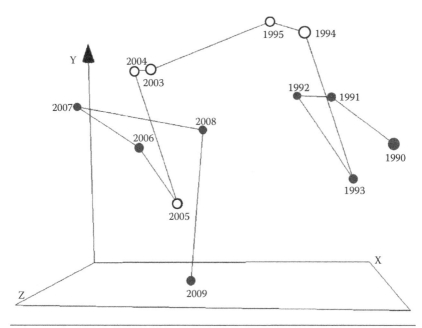

Figure 7.7 Federal Government Approval (1990–2009): Virtual reality space with Sammon's mapping. Colors indicate the political party in power during the given year: white = Liberal, black = Conservative (colors were chosen at random). Lines join subsequent years.

in Figure 7.7. Its first notable feature is that the overall structure is composed of two separated clumps of objects, (1990–1993) and (2006–2009), located at the two extremes of the X-axis, corresponding to the two periods of Conservative government. They are separated by an elongated chain of objects (1994–2005) corresponding to the period when the Liberal Party was in power. This overall structure is similar to the one found in the space obtained for the Federal Government Spending in between 1987 and 2010 (Figure 7.2). This is very interesting because, on the one hand, the two data sets have different descriptor variables (i.e., polls addressing different topics), and on the other hand, the values of these variables are heterogeneous. They are scalar, real-valued in the case of spending (in other words, without uncertainty) and interval-valued in the case of approval (indicating a range of possible values, instead of one with certitude).

The changes of opinion with time are shown in Figure 7.8. As with the case of government spending, the pattern defined by the trends is also similar. However, notable differences are that changes of opinion are more frequent and also that they move in opposite directions.

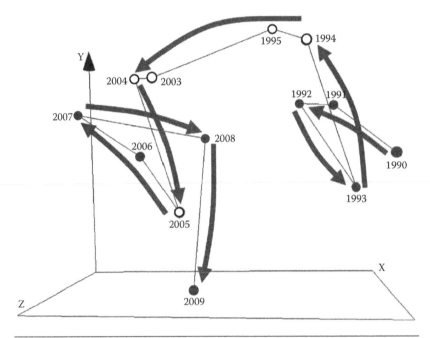

Figure 7.8 Federal Government Approval (1990–2009): Virtual reality space with Sammon's mapping. Colors indicate the political party in power during the given year: white = Liberal, black = Conservative (colors were chosen at random). Arrows indicate trends in opinion change.

Two subsets of data corresponding to the years where the Conservative party came to power are clearly differentiated in Figure 7.8 (black spheres). They correspond to 1990–1993 and 2006–2009. Their separation in the virtual reality space indicates that the pooled subpopulation perceived these two periods of the same political party as very dissimilar (from the point of view of the elements used in the pool for characterizing federal government approval). In addition, their policies induce frequent changes of opinion, some of them in opposite directions. These patterns could be seen as a signature of the Conservative governments covered by the 1990–2009 polls. In the case of the Liberals, only one period in power is covered. At the beginning of their mandate (1994) the people's perception is not too different, from the one characterizing the Conservative period (1990–1993, right hand side of the virtual reality space). However, the opinion about the Liberal policies steadily drifts without reversals, toward levels of approval quite similar to those expressed about the second Conservative government (2006–2009, left hand side of the space). At the end of their mandate, the opinion about their policies ends up being very different than the ones at the beginning of their term. A large contrast between the beginning and the end, with a continuous, one-directional drift in between, was the signature of the Liberal government. The time period covered by the data does not include a second Liberal government, thus making it impossible to examine the change of opinion between two Liberal periods, as was possible with the Conservatives.

From political and sociological points of view, it is natural to wonder whether the citizens' opinions about the government, as contained in polls' data, support the hypothesis of a sharp differentiation between the two major Canadian parties from the point of view of the policies that they put in place. Figure 7.9, which is the same space as the one from Figure 7.7, but from another, rotated perspective, proves that this indeed is the case. It shows a clear separation between a left region, composed of all years of Conservative government (both periods), and a right one, composed of all years of Liberal government. If the problem

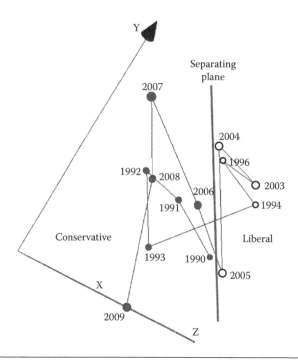

Figure 7.9 Federal Government Approval (1990–2009): another perspective of Figure 7.7 showing how the nonlinear mapping produces a clear, linear separation between the classes defined by the two political parties (class membership information was not used in the computation of the virtual reality space).

would have been formulated as a binary classification one (hence, supervised), with the two political parties as the classes to differentiate, the nonlinear space resulting from the unsupervised problem formulation would be one where these classes turn out to be *linearly* separable.

Conclusions

Visualization approaches based on VR representations of unsupervised, nonlinear, lower-dimensional spaces are appropriate and effective tools for the analysis and exploration of government data. Examples from two real-world cases composed of opinion polls data about Canadian Federal Government Spending and about Federal Government Approval, with respect to social and economic policies, proved that these visualization techniques are suitable in the presence of heterogeneous information as well. In the two studied cases, the descriptor variables belong to different data types: one data set was composed of crisp variables (with absolute certainty), and the other data set was composed of variables with interval values (expressing answers with uncertainty).

Visual data exploration and mining with these spaces are particularly useful operations at the initial stages of the analytics, where they can quickly provide insights about the structure of the information, regularities, oddities, changes, trends, and other events. However, they can also be used at any stage of the process, including the analysis of results produced by other data analytics procedures. The example data sets analyzed were purposely chosen as small ones in order to better illustrate the possibilities of the discussed visual approaches. They can be scaled up in Big Data and the IoT scenarios, where their possibilities and usefulness grow considerably.

References

1. J.W. Tukey. *Exploratory Data Analysis. Reading*, MA: Addison-Wesley publishing, 1977.
2. F. Mosteller and J.W. Tukey. *Data Analysis and Regression.* Reading, MA: Addison-Wesley publishing, 1977.
3. D.C. Hoaglin, F. Mosteller, and J.W. Tukey. *Understanding Robust and Exploratory Data Analysis.* New York: John Wiley and Sons, 1983.

4. D.C. Hoaglin, F. Mosteller, and J.W. Tukey. *Exploring Data Tables, Trends, and Shapes.* New York: John Wiley and Sons, 1985.

5. J.J. Valdés. Virtual reality representation of relational systems and decision rules: An exploratory tool for understanding data structure. In P. Hajek (ed.), *Theory and Application of Relational Structures as Knowledge Instruments,* Prague, Czech Republic, November 2002. Meeting of the COST Action274.

6. J.J. Valdés. Virtual reality representation of information systems and decision rules: An exploratory tool for understanding data and knowledge. In G. Wang, Q. Liu, Y. Yao, and A. Skowron (eds.), *Proceedings of the 9-th International Conference on Rough Sets, Fuzzy Sets, Data Mining and Granular Computing,* volume Lecture Notes in Artificial Intelligence LNAI 2639, pp. 615–618, Chongqing, China, October 2003. Springer-Verlag.

7. J.J. Valdés. Visual data mining of astronomic data with virtual reality spaces: Understanding the structure of large data sets. In *Proceedings of the XIV ADASS International Conference on Astronomical Data Analysis Software & Systems XIV,* Vol. 347, pp. 51–59, Pasadena, CL, October 24–27, 2004. Astronomical Society of the Pacific Conference Series.

8. S. Card. *The Human-Computer Interaction Handbook: Fundamentals, Evolving Technologies, and Emerging Applications.* A. Sears, and J.A. Jacko (eds.). Mahwah, NJ: Lawrence Erlbaum Associates, 2007.

9. M. Averbuch. As you like it: Tailorable information visualization. Technical report, Database Visualization Research Group, Tufts University, 2004.

10. C. Chen. Top 10 unsolved information visualization problems. *IEEE Computer Graphics and Applications,* 25(4):12–16, 2005.

11. L.A. Zadeh. Fuzzy sets. *Information and Control,* 8(3):338–353, 1965.

12. Z. Pawlak. Rough sets. *International Journal of Parallel Programming,* 11(5):341–356, 1982.

13. Dempster. Upper and lower probabilities induced by a multivalued mapping. *Annals of Mathematical Statistics,* 38(2):325–339, 1967.

14. G. Shafer. *A Mathematical Theory of Evidence.* Princeton, NJ: Princeton University Press, 1976.

15. W. Pedrycz. Shadowed sets: Representing and processing fuzzy sets. *IEEE Transactions on Systems, Man, and Cybernetics Part B: Cybernetics,* 28(1):103–109, 1998.

16. M. Tory and T. Möller. Human factors in visualization research. *IEEE Transactions on Visualization and Computer Graphics,* 10(1):72–84, 2004.

17. R. Voigt. *An Extended Scatterplot Matrix and Case Studies in Information Visualization.* PhD thesis, Hochschule Magdeburg-Stendal, 2002.

18. S.J. Simoff, M.H. Bhlen, and A. Mazeika (eds.). *Visual Data Mining: Theory, Techniques and Tools for Visual Analytics.* Berlin, Germany: Springer, 2008.

19. J.J. Valdés, E. Romero, and A.J. Barton. Data and knowledge visualization with virtual reality spaces, neural networks and rough sets: Application to cancer and geophysical prospecting. *Expert Systems with Applications,* 39(18):13193–13201, 2012.

20. R. Bellman. *Adaptive Control Processes: A Guided Tour.* Princeton, NJ: Princeton University Press, 1961.
21. F. Camastra and A. Staiano. Intrinsic dimension estimation: Advances and open problems. *Information Sciences*, 328:2641, 2016.
22. E. Levina and P.J. Bickel. Maximum likelihood estimation of intrinsic dimension. *Advances in Neural Information Processing Systems*, 17:777–784, 2005.
23. P. Grassberger and I. Procaccia. Measuring the strangeness of strange attractors. *Physica,* D(9):189–208, 1983.
24. P. Grassberger and I. Procaccia. Geodesic entropic graphs for dimension and entropy estimation in manifold learning. *IEEE Transactions on Signal Processing*, 52(8):2210–2221, 2004.
25. J. Kruskal. Nonmetric multidimensional scaling: A numerical method. *Psychometrika*, 29:115–129, 1964.
26. J. Kruskal. Multidimensional scaling by optimizing goodness of fit to a nonmetric hypothesis. *Psychometrika*, 29(1):1–27, 1964.
27. I.I. Borg and P. Groenen. *Modern Multidimensional Scaling - Theory and Applications.* Springer Series in Statistics, New York: Springer, 1997.
28. J.W. Sammon. A nonlinear mapping for data structure analysis. *IEEE Transactions on Computers,* C- 18(5):401–409, 1969.
29. W. Press, B. Flannery, S. Teukolsky, and W. Vetterling. *Numeric Recipes in C.* New York: Cambridge University Press, 1992.
30. J.J. Valdés and A.J. Barton. Multi-objective evolutionary optimization for constructing neural networks for virtual reality visual data mining: Application to geophysical prospecting. *Neural Networks*, 20(4):498–508, 2007.
31. L.J.P. van der Maaten and G. Hinton. Visualizing high-dimensional data using t-sne. *Journal of Machine Learning Research*, 9:2579–2605, 2008.
32. G.E . Hinton and S.T. Roweis. Stochastic neighbor embedding. *Advances in Neural Information Processing Systems*, 15:833–840, 2002.
33. J.J. Valdés, C. Cheung, and M. Li. Sensor dynamics in high dimensional phase spaces via nonlinear transformations: Application to helicopter loads monitoring. In 2014 *IEEE Symposium Series on Computational Intelligence (IEEE SSCI 2014),* Caribe Royale Convention Center, Orlando, FL, December 9–12, 2014. IEEE.
34. J.J. Valdés, F.A. Alsulaiman, and A. El Saddik. Visualization of Handwritten Signatures based on Haptic Information. In R. Abielmona et al. (eds.), *Recent Advances of Computational Intelligence in Defense and Security.* Studies in Computational Intelligence 621. Switzerland: Springer International Publishing, 2016.
35. Canadian Opinion Research Archive at Queen's University (CORA). http://www.queensu.ca/cora/.
36. Canadian Opinion Research Archive at Queen's University. Trends. http://www.queensu.ca/cora/3trends.html.

8

INSTITUTIONALIZING ANALYTICS

A Case Study

GREGORY RICHARDS, CATHERINE ELLIOTT, AND SWEE C. GOH

Contents

Introduction

The organization that is the subject of this case study is an educational institution with a budget of more than $20 billion, spanning a geographical region of more than 200,000 square miles. At the time of the research, the organization had been engaged in the processes to be described for more than 7 years, so much of what we learned was retrospective and based on a long-enough period of time to generate valuable lessons learned.

Data for the case study were collected through several sources. First, we performed a review of relevant documentation that included reports, plans, presentations, and academic papers. Second, we conducted semi-structured interviews with 15 key informants in the organization, including the senior management team. In this report, we will explain the genesis of the organization's approach to analytics, the process, and the steps taken, and then, we will discuss the results achieved. The organization would prefer to remain anonymous; accordingly, any data that might identify the organization have been excluded from this report. The quotes have also been adjusted from their original verbatim report, but they convey the meaning of the original. This will not detract from the story of institutionalizing analytics, which includes four main initiatives: (1) clarifying expected outcomes, (2) identifying and managing the data thought to be useful for these outcomes, (3) building capacity, and (4) learning from analytics.

Governance and Leadership

One of the seemingly unrelated factors that, in our view, was a tremendous help to the institutionalization of analytics was the fact that senior managers gained consensus and buy-in on three key strategic outcomes for the entire organization. Once this was done, it rapidly became apparent to the senior team that the accomplishment of these goals and indeed their ability to continually move the yardsticks, so to speak, could be greatly enhanced through the use of the volumes of data being gathered by the organization.

An important point here is that the declaration of strategic outcomes was not enough to clarify strategy for such a large, regionalized organization. Each region or division needed to translate these outcomes into clear deliverables at different levels in the organization. Some regions adopted the use of balanced scorecards, while other regions used logic models. The senior team provided leeway to the divisions to adopt whatever approach made sense. Some regions decided to use the balanced scorecard framework adapted to the educational environment. Informants reported that the use of the scorecard provided a means for staff to have conversations about priorities related to the strategic outcomes. At the end of the scorecard development process, managers were clear on what specifically needed to be done in their work units to meet strategic priorities. In addition, the scorecard development process enabled staff to be more selective about projects; those that did not advance the overall strategy were often eliminated.

Other branches used logic models that are common in the field of evaluation. In this case, the conversations tended to focus on inputs and outputs and how these linked to the desired strategic outcomes. The result was similar to that noted by regions using balanced scorecards: clarity about the work of the unit and its relationship to the strategic outcomes, and the ability to focus on activities that drove results.

At the corporate level, many initiatives were put in place to coordinate the various plans being put in place. A strategic dashboard was created to report on substantive initiatives. Accompanying the dashboard was an *Initiative Monitor*. This monitor included information on legislation, policy, budget priorities, programs, and initiatives. It also listed important data for tracking progress on specific initiatives (e.g., project lead, start date, end date, and outcomes). Most importantly, the monitor addressed alignment of these initiatives with the organization's core priorities and targets. This information was used on a regular basis to avoid duplication and redundancy in different divisions and branches. It was also used on an annual basis for strategic and operational planning.

The various plans and initiatives were rolled up in a central repository that helped monitor all key initiatives that supported the strategic outcomes. To provide support and central coordination, teams that focused on different functional areas were created. For example, one might focus on admissions' processing and the other might focus on graduation rates. An extensive training program was delivered to help everyone involved understand both the system and the processes involved in making it work. Updated quarterly (or monthly for important issues or meetings), the monitor was a key element in helping to keep senior managers on track.

Finally, dashboards and scorecards are more useful when targets are available. To formulate these targets, the managers relied heavily on research and lessons learned from other jurisdictions and other countries, when necessary. International standards were adopted where these existed, and where such standards were not available, the organization would develop its own standards, based on the experience of managers in trial and error in some cases. The importance of this benchmarking approach was to provide objective data with which to establish targets, thus defusing the sometimes-endless debates that could happen in organizations related to this issue.

In summary, the time and effort spent on clarifying the strategic outcomes enabled departmental managers to fully understand how the work they were doing led to accomplishment of the strategic outcomes. The various tools that were adopted helped define the type of data needed for monitoring progress and for assessing the impact of activities on the desired outcomes. This is an important point, because the foundational nature of analytics in organizations is helping managers understand whether the activities on which they are spending resources lead to the outcomes they care about. By continually testing these activity–outcome relationships, managers can explore new ways of meeting outcomes within their budget constraints. Figure 8.1 provides a simplified view of the steps involved in ensuring that strategic outcomes were translated to all regions and divisions across the organizations. A key and common theme is the inclusion of *human elements* in the form of the functional teams that helped ensure continuous coordination and communication.

Managing the Data Supply Chain

The use of data in an organization calls for a well-developed data supply chain (DSC). A typical DSC needs data capture, storage, transformation, and dissemination tools. Data must, of course, be

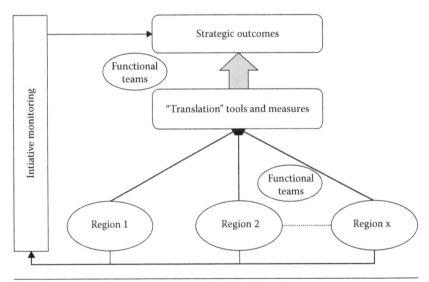

Figure 8.1   Model for institutionalization of Big Data and Analytics.

available, but they also must be transformed and *cleaned* to make sure that they can be used properly for analysis. Furthermore, if managers do not trust the quality of the data, the analytic effort will stall.

This organization already collected a significant amount of data: student admission rates, graduation rates, student performance data, and surveys from students and other stakeholders. The emphasis then was on ensuring that data could be made available to decision makers in a useful form. To support the drive toward improved student achievement and development of an evidence-based culture, the department launched the *Evidence-based Student Achievement Process* (ESAP) managed and supported by a Statistics and Analysis branch. It focused on building capacity, both at the corporate level and across the regions. The objective was to build skills in the areas of data management, technology, and data use. The ESAP supported regions that were undertaking data management activities (i.e., data accuracy, timeliness, and relevance), which are critical to the precise tracking of student progress and planning of effective instructional strategies for improved student outcomes. It also provided support to regions developing technology related to the implementation of local decision-support tools and reporting.

As a support to the ESAP, in 2005, seven regional networks were created to help connect learning communities. Working collaboratively with the corporate team, regional networks connected across the vast geographic regions to develop and share professional learning resources, deliver learning events, share effective practices, and forge connections to the research community in support of improved student outcomes. Along the way, the flow of information from corporate to and among regions also helped identify issues and problems to refine ESAP.

A key accomplishment of ESAP was the creation of a web-enabled system for collecting and managing elementary and secondary education-related data. Data are collected three times per year (October, March, and June) and integrated across regions and school boards. The level of detail is impressive: information is available down to a class in a specific school. Data are validated and verified at source, improving data accuracy and integrity. The overall purpose of this application is to gather more accurate and reliable data, protected by privacy legislation and a rigorously controlled security system. These

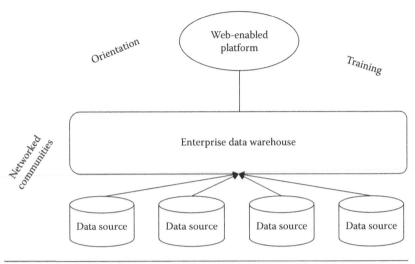

Figure 8.2   The data management process.

data are subsequently stored, integrated, and anonymized in an enterprise data warehouse (EDW), where it is utilized to develop and promote information practices for analysis, policy development, and evidence-based decision making in the education sector.

The EDW is important for the delivery of near-real-time information to managers. Like many jurisdictions around the world, this department administers standardized tests. However, these are done at fixed times during the year and at certain grades. The EDW provides an ongoing source of information on student progress, thus allowing managers to compare schools, link in-class performance with results on standardized tests, and, thus, adjust teaching protocols to better encourage student success.

In addition, the EDW has enabled development of a tool for parents that provides information about schools in terms of student performance. These data are available, on the web, for all parents to access and use. Figure 8.2 provides a diagrammatic view of the data sources available to the organization.

Learning from Analytics

The analytics process within the department is used to learn what works and what does not. Based on this, managers adjust the overall strategy and create new initiatives, as needed. Analytics also contributes to accountability and resource allocation. The reports generated using data also serves an important communication function, providing information to the public and other stakeholder groups.

For the above to occur, one of the characteristics of the system, the glue that enables it to drive performance, is leadership that encourages continual improvement. Therefore, while the strategy maybe well formulated, the metrics well defined and agreed upon, and the analyses well conducted, it is the actual implementation that makes it all resonate and work together. The right levels of resources and expertise are also important, and it is the organizational leaders that have the authority to provide these resources.

One respondent clarified the point that *a heavy emphasis on the people* aspect was needed: first, providing training and technical support, so that teachers and others within the system could use data and truly embrace the notion of continuous improvement; second, making it politically OK to use evidence to generate positive change. As the participant explained:

> So in my view it's not the data or the metrics or measurements as much as it is about the degree to which people can be assisted and supported in responding to those metrics.

In terms of using data for strategic adjustments, the senior team meets regularly to review progress. At these meetings, the performance data from the EDW and from other sources are reviewed.

By comparing results against the key targets, managers can estimate progress toward the three priorities and discuss any critical issues that need adjustment. The review allows the team to ensure that the organization is working together across different divisions toward a common goal. As this respondent describes:

> The head of the organization uses these meetings to keep a handle on what's going on, and he gets to chew on the challenges to see where he personally needs to step in.

Operationally, there is a constant balancing and re-balancing and continual shifting of tactics, based on the information generated by the analytics process. For example, a new program was launched to target schools that were in the middle of the performance range expected. The data showed that lower-performing schools had been reduced from 19% to 5%. Then, the task was how to raise the level of performance across all schools, leading to the launch of the new program.

Data are also used to make difficult decisions about resource allocation and about which programs should be allocated more money because of evidence being brought to bear on the problem. In most cases, having results forces more rigor and focus behind the process as well. This participant described the utilization of data:

> Obviously to ensure that we're on track for whatever we are doing, making decisions on resource allocation. You know, are we getting value for money? Are we wasting money here? Should we spend more money or less money on this? FTE's, which are our staff, should we move resources here, should we have fewer or more?

In fact, the overall funding formula for the department is based on data. There are more than 10 factors that are taken into consideration (e.g., factors such as geography, size, and so on), and these factors are fed into a formula, which determines the money allocated to different regions.

These data also serve an important accountability function, since the three outcomes represent policy commitments that the government has made to taxpayers. As a result, reports generated from the data can be potentially controversial. Therefore, the department has put a lot of work into ensuring credibility of the data used at all levels. The fact that the head of the organization and the minister were heavily invested in the strategic outcomes—politically and personally—means that everyone is aware of the need to be transparent about what was working and what was not.

> There was high priority and focus on the three outcomes. Senior leadership would pay close attention to progress reports and ask for evidence probe, often asking "So what next? How are you going to improve?" Then, at the next meeting, we would be faced with follow-up questions.

At the individual level, data have also been used effectively to change the nature of performance appraisal discussions. The focus was on results and not so much on what people were doing on a daily basis. Clearly, in a government organization, procedures must be respected, but the message being sent was that the leadership trusted that people in the organization were aware of procedure, and the question was more about what was being delivered.

Finally, credible data, when used properly, can aid in communicating with stakeholder groups.

Unions, school administrators, parents, and politicians, all get the same information from a common database. This is a powerful means of creating a level playing field for problem solving. Although not all stakeholders always agree on the changes needed, the data provide a common base from which to start discussions.

Overall, we can see that the core elements were established to promote learning from data. An important point to consider here is that the use of analytics should lead to change. In addition, change, especially in large, complex public-sector agencies is not always easy. The key strategies adopted by this organization were dissemination of results and the use of external experts, where needed, to bolster internal findings. For example, reports created by the internal analytics team would be summarized in online videos distributed through the organization's intranet. Then, the feedback would be gathered from interested stakeholder, and where necessary, external researchers would be called in to examine the internal findings in detail and provide objective commentary. Once all this information was understood by organizational members, the change process could begin. It is instructive to note that although many organizations are investing in analytics, few have thought through how the data would be used in driving continuous improvement. It is an important step, because without the ability to change, the investments in analytics would be wasted.

Challenges

Implementation of a data-driven management approach across such a large organization is not without its challenges. Alignment was one of the first issues faced by the senior leadership team. This included corporate and regional work units. At the corporate level, one of the questions concerned the roles and decision-making authorities of the various functional teams created to help coordinate the strategic focus and operational activities. At the regional level, the issue was one of horizontal coordination among the different organizational units. The senior leadership team was aware of these alignment issues and was therefore deliberate about concentrating on alignment as a key result area. Accordingly, they created precise, simple goals; they placed a strong emphasis on consultation and communication; they were consistent in terms of expectations; and they built organizational linkages into the system to enable communication across different functional areas.

From a broader perspective, one of the most fundamental challenges was the need to change the belief system of various stakeholders. First was the notion of the strategic outcomes themselves, which assumed that all students could excel, regardless of their socioeconomic background. Second, the organization needed to evolve people's perception of evidence and how it could be used. There were some definitional issues around the metrics that needed to be addressed (what constitutes valid evidence, an appropriate measure, etc.) and some skepticism about the metrics. These aspects were handled by providing continual training and development, by working with external objective parties such as universities and other educational institutions, and by ensuring that leadership at all levels in the organization followed a common approach that included not only a focus on results but also a respect for staff and a willingness to listen.

As pointed out by many of the respondents, the focus on training and development was critical because lack of capacity in the system was commonly mentioned barrier to change. There was a tremendous need for professional development to raise the competence across the system, at all levels and all sectors. This included the creation of new processes, development of competencies of staff to work with, and making decisions with data. The focus on obtaining external objective evidence, where necessary, was also an important element of the process. Leadership worked hard to dispel the *not invented here* syndrome, so that managers felt comfortable using external resources to help with training and development, interpretation of results, or conduction of additional research, as needed, depending on the results of the internal analysis.

Access to data was a barrier at first. As mentioned earlier in this report, the organization had a lot of data but needed to spend the time and effort necessary to make the data accessible in a usable format to users. To be able to get resources to do so depended on the business case demonstrating how the use of data could contribute to better results. To acquire additional resources, once the program was up and running, it called for a demonstration of results. The department was able to show progress toward the policy objectives, a situation that made it easier for managers to argue for additional resources.

Conclusions

According to interviewees, the overall approach to outcome management has contributed to strategic focus, to the ability to modify initiatives based on evidence, to motivate other stakeholders, and to build engagement and shared responsibility.

Strategic Focus

The approach has provided a sound platform for discussion about the organization's strategy and how each division and region contributes to achieving the core priorities. This focus is felt at all levels of the organization, from the political level to the senior administrative leadership, departmental employees, and other stakeholders. It has helped clarify many discussions, by focusing on the degree to which investments in new initiatives lead to accomplishment of the three main outcomes. This aspect is supported by the use of analytics, but it was clear that in the absence of this clear strategic focus, the use of analytics would not be as effective.

Mid-Course Adjustments

Because of the consistent focus on key priorities and goals, clear metrics, and regular reporting mechanisms, the leadership teams (at all levels) are able to *revise and adapt the strategies, to make decisions about what's working more or less.* A continuous process of analysis—comparison of different schools, different student segments, different programming strategies, and so on—is providing a wealth of evidence permitting managers and others within the system to try out new ideas. The point here is that risk is managed because everyone is aware that any new idea needs to be outcome-focused and that data will be available to monitor the relative success of these new approaches. Those that are successful will receive additional investment. Those that fail will be abandoned.

Motivation

Several participants mentioned that the overall process has been very motivational for employees. Having consistent goals, strategies, measures, and targets to shoot for has served to catalyze employees' energies. By *staying the course* over many years, following through on commitments, providing resources, and permitting experimentation where needed, a feeling of goodwill and trust developed throughout the organization. Perhaps, most importantly, all employees and stakeholders can easily see that the progress is being made against ambitious targets. These targets were a *stretch* from the outset, and even so, the no one in the organization has not backed down or resorted to *gaming of measures*. The overall philosophy has been to manage by reality: let the data speak, so that we can all adjust as needed. In this way, he has slowly gained the teachers' trust. As this senior executive notes, it has also been motivating for the management team.

> Many of my direct reports, particularly at the Director level find themselves fully engaged, work is meaningful and they know that they have the support of senior management.

Engagement and Shared Accountability

Thinking strategically about how to communicate effectively and how to stimulate dialogue with the many groups throughout the sector has promoted an ongoing conversation. Partially, this is a result of the level of trust generated, since senior leadership is willing to manage by reality. In addition, the fact that all the data are available to everyone promotes clarity in conversations among and between the various stakeholders. As this senior manager explains:

> This strong sense of engagement promotes conversations at all levels. Everybody has monthly check-ins to look at what we're doing well and not doing well.

This active dialogue with stakeholder groups has also served to engender a deeper level of commitment to results, and this goes a long way toward creating a sense of shared responsibility and accountability. For those who are less intimately involved (e.g., the broader public), performance data are also necessary to fulfill political and fiduciary obligations.

> As a public servant I can now report to the politicians to say here is where we are relative to the mandate we were given. It's been useful because we can show that we take seriously the investments made and the trust shown in our department.

The approach taken by this organization ultimately promotes development of a virtuous cycle, as shown in Figure 8.3. The key point is that none of the practices adopted by the organization would be successful if the other factors noted in the figure were not in place. It takes enlightened, outcomes-focused leadership who will accept the need for using data as a key asset in the delivery of the mandate. Development of a culture of management by reality is also required along with investment in training and development, so that people within the system are comfortable using data. At the same time, processes that focus on accountability and the democratization of decision rights to the manager closest to the action, so to speak, must be developed, deployed, and sustained. With these factors in place, the virtuous cycle will emerge.

In this cycle, all employees and stakeholders are fully engaged in delivering on their individual mandates, because they can see how they promote the outcomes that everyone care about. In addition, they have access to interim knowledge of results: the data provide

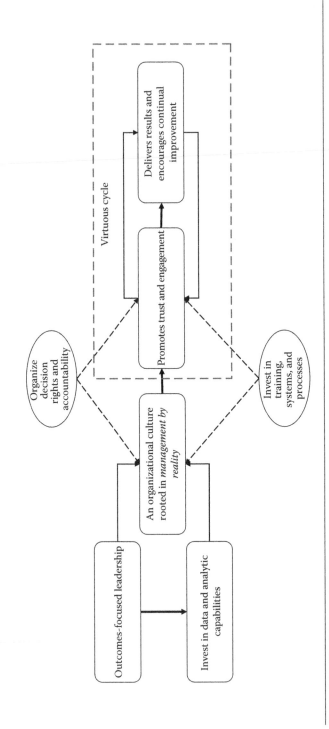

Figure 8.3 The virtuous cycle.

evidence about successes and failures. This, in turn, promotes continual improvement, which reinforces trust and engagement. Some organizations have been able to create such virtuous cycles in specific work units or responsibility centers. It is rare for large public-sector organizations to do so however. The cornerstone for this organization was the coordination between the political and departmental leaderships, the fact that leaders at both levels *demonstrated* attention and interest in outcomes and a willingness to invest strategically in people, tools, and systems to enable continual performance improvement.

9

MODELING DATA SOURCES

OKHAIDE AKHIGBE AND DANIEL AMYOT

Contents

Introduction

Data are supposed to be used in the service of accomplishing business goals. Managers would therefore benefit from understanding the data sources available to support specific types of decision making. Frameworks exist for enterprise architecture design. They link information systems (ISs) to business requirements, but from an analytics perspective, little is understood about how data sources are linked to business objectives and to specific types of decisions. In this paper, we introduce a framework that establishes links between an organization's business goals and its IS. The framework relies on the User Requirements Notation (URN) (Amyot and Mussbacher, 2011; Amyot et al., 2012) and jUCMNav (Amyot et al., 2012), a free Eclipse-based tool for analyzing and managing URN models, to model business scenarios, the stakeholders involved, their intentions in terms of organizational objectives, tasks they perform, and the IS that supports these objectives.

The URN is the first international standard to combine goal modeling (the Goal-oriented Requirement Language [GRL]) with scenario modeling (the Use Case Map notation [UCM]) (Amyot and Mussbacher, 2011; Mussbacher and Amyot, 2009) to provide a conceptual view of what capabilities and architectures are required to accomplish organizational objectives. It also facilitates the identification of capabilities, services, and architectures needed to fulfill stakeholder goals.

This approach is valuable in that it can permit managers and IT professionals to anticipate the impact on business decision making related to addition or removal of a specific technology. Moreover, it clarifies for decision makers the existence and overall quality of their data sources. In addition, the outcome of the mapping process leads to a better understanding of the role of data for managerial decision making. The remainder of this paper will describe the overall process and then conclude with an applied scenario from a public-sector organization in which a portion of its business objectives was mapped to underlying data sources.

Background

The approach taken to fully leverage the advantage of the mapping process is to create both an *as-is scenario* and a *to-be scenario*. That is, managers and IT professionals work together to map the current system. The mapping process includes defining business goals, the data sources that support decision-making about these goals, and the relative quality of the data and the ISs. Where gaps are defined, the *to-be scenario* is created, which provides guidance for both the manager and the IT professionals about evolution of the IT system and the consequent decision-making capabilities. For the purposes of this paper, we will examine a subset of the organization to provide a simplified view of the process.

As discussed earlier, the modeling approach combines two sublanguages, GRL for modeling actors and their intentions and UCM for describing scenarios/processes and architectures. Without getting too much into the details, four primary concepts are defined during the methodology: *intentional elements* goals (quantitatively expressed), softgoals (qualitatively expressed and may include task, resource, and beliefs), *indicators* (or key performance indicators [KPIs]), *intentional links* (such as contributions, correlations, dependencies, and decompositions), and *actors* (basically various forms of stakeholders, or the system itself).

Actors, which represent the system or stakeholders, are represented in GRL with ⬭. Actors contain GRL intentional elements such as goals ⟨Goal⟩, softgoals ⟨Softgoal⟩, tasks ⟨Task⟩, and resources ▭Resource. These elements are connected to other GRL intentional elements through links such as AND/OR decompositions ⊢—, contributions ⟶, correlation ┈┈⟶, and dependencies ⟶▪⟶.

One important step in creating this scenario is to decide about the relative importance of organizational objectives. In addition to the complexity of processes at play within enterprises, modelers have to take into consideration techno-social (Hoogervorst, 2004) and political factors related to prioritizing objectives, taking actions, using ISs, or handling changes that arise in the organization.

Finding suitable trade-offs to satisfy multiple conflicting factors can be done through multi-criteria decision-making approaches. One such approach is the analytic hierarchy process (AHP), which has been used in a wide variety of different decision-making situations (Saaty, 1988, 1990). We use AHP to evaluate and obtain importance levels and priorities of the various business objectives. Since organizations deal with multiple objectives, it might not be possible to map all of them. The outcome of AHP enables decisions about which objectives should be mapped or which take priority in terms of preserving specific sources of data. The steps utilized are the following:

1. Develop a pairwise comparison matrix for each business objective's importance level or priority.
2. Normalize the matrix.
3. Average the value in each row to get the corresponding rating.

The result is as shown in Table 9.1. The row averages provide a ranking out of 100 of the various objectives (A through C). Because we use a ranking of 0–100 for GRL contribution and importance levels, we multiply each row average by 100.

Table 9.1   Calculated Importance Level of Each Goal Relative to the Other

	GOAL A	GOAL B	GOAL C	ROW AVERAGE	MULTIPLIED BY 100
Goal A	0.23	0.22	0.33	0.26	26
Goal B	0.69	0.65	0.56	0.63	63
Goal C	0.08	0.13	0.11	0.11	11
Sum	1	1	1	1	100

The Modeling Scenario

Based on the discussions that we had with personnel (a director, a business architect, the technical architect, and project managers) in the organization (which we will refer to as OrgA) responsible for their enterprise architecture, the Grants and Contributions Program (G&C) was selected as the target for this research. This program provides funding to third parties to carry out activities within the mandate OrgA. At the time, this organization was implementing and addressing enterprise architecture–related concerns. A number of manual processes related to the G&C were being automated, and regional operations were working to integrate their processes with headquarters; therefore, the timing was appropriate for experimentation with the mapping approach.

The business goal-modeling step involved identifying the stakeholders, goals, softgoals, and tasks involved in this process. We used the pairwise comparison technique described earlier to compute the importance levels of intentional elements and contribution weights, using a set of questionnaires.

An important point is that satisfaction of business owners is measured at each layer to help define potential relationships between and among the various goals, tasks, and the IS. The various components of the IS are evaluated according to six characteristics defined as follows (Delone and McLean, 2002, 2003).

- *System quality*: Indicates characteristics such as reliability, flexibility, ease of learning, sophistication, and feature of intuitiveness.
- *Information quality*: Indicates characteristics of the IS output such as relevance, understandability, accuracy, completeness, and usability.

- *Service quality*: Indicates whether the quality of support that the system users receive from IT personnel is responsive, accurate, reliable, provided with empathy, and so on.
- *System use*: Indicates the degree and manner that all stakeholders utilize the capabilities of the IS in terms of amount of usage, frequency of use, nature of use, appropriateness of use, extent of use, purpose of use, and so on.
- *User satisfaction*: Indicates the users' level of satisfaction with reports, websites, and data that they get from the IS.
- *Net benefits*: Indicates the extent to which the IS contributes to the success of individuals, groups, and organizations that use it, in terms of improved decision making, improved productivity, increased sales, cost reduction, and so on.

All evaluations are done by the managers and others involved in the processes. Figure 9.1 depicts the overall framework that includes actors, goals, and linkages. The actor *Grant Allocation Department* has a softgoal *Implement Grants Program* that has to be satisfied at 100%. The *as-is* evaluation suggests that it is currently at 64%. Similar evaluations and expectations can be seen for the actors Program Officer, Accountant, and Information System. The assessment of the quality of IS can be seen in below IS 1 and IS 2, each of which contributes 50% to the tasks of the Program Officer and Accountant.

Figure 9.2 provides an ideal scenario model that is used as a baseline to create a gap analysis. Figure 9.3 shows the results of the gap analysis, where the improvement needed is shown in angle brackets (< >) across the diagram.

Adaptation

Organizations are not static: they have to adapt to continuous internal and external changes. New tasks might be needed, for example, or ISs might be retired or become unavailable. To reflect the impact of these types of changes, the framework allows for continuous scenario modeling. That is, once the system has been set up in the software tool, additions, deletions, or modifications of any of the elements can be automatically assessed. For example, Figure 9.4 shows the adjustments made if IS 1 no longer contributes to the *assess grants project* task

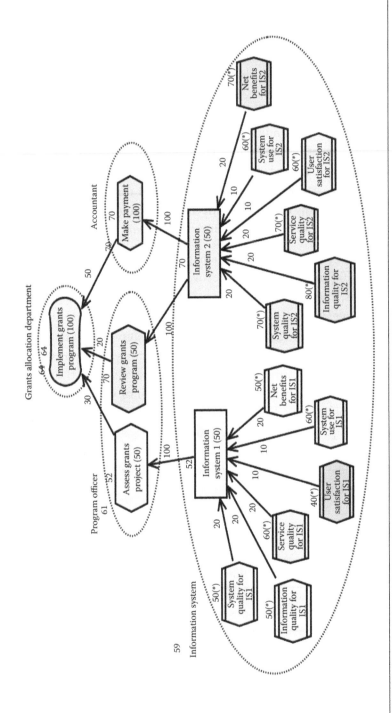

Figure 9.1 Example as-is scenario.

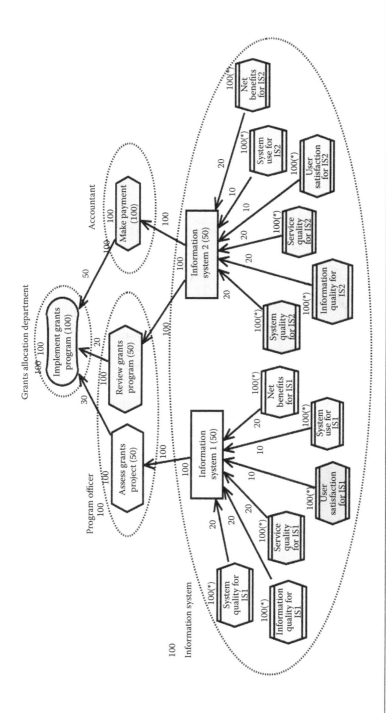

Figure 9.2 Example ideal scenario.

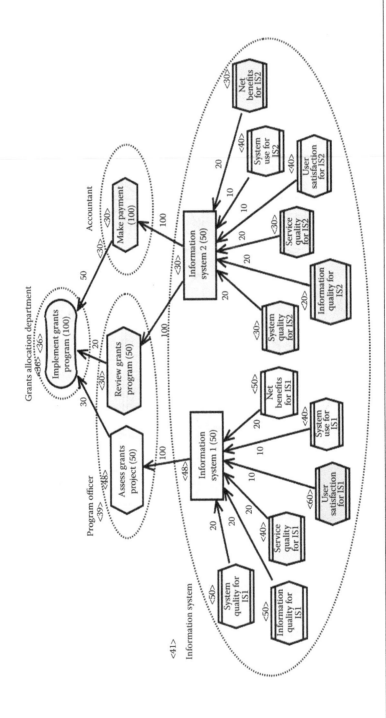

Figure 9.3 Example gap analysis.

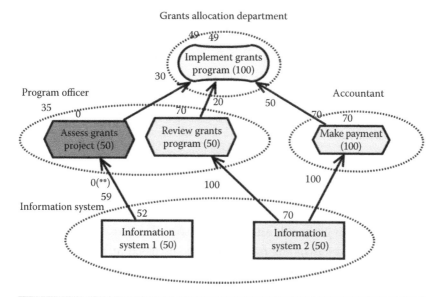

Figure 9.4 Deletion of contribution link from information system 1.

of the Program Officer. Satisfaction levels drop from 61 to 35, and as a consequence, the Grants Allocation Department's overall satisfaction would drop from 64 to 49.

Tasks might also be added at different levels in the system to better meet requirements. For example, in Figure 9.5, we see addition of the *Review Payments* task. The Grant Allocation Department's satisfaction

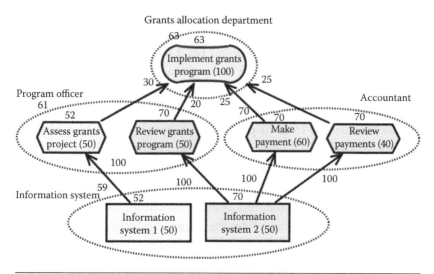

Figure 9.5 Addition of a new task.

level drops marginally from 64 to 63 in this case, suggesting that the new task has a negligible effect on overall satisfaction. Satisfaction might drop because the new task slows down the distribution of grants, and so, this scenario would necessarily call for a reassessment of the goals of the department. For example, managers might need to reconsider the relative importance of speed versus accuracy in the *Make Payment* task.

Evaluation of the Usefulness of the Mapping Framework

The evaluation was based on Yu et al. (2012), and it included anonymous responses gathered from senior personnel in OrgA who had been working with the mapping framework. As discussed in Yu et al. (2012), the evaluation of an enterprise architecture framework should focus on what the framework does and what issues the framework encompasses. Accordingly, questions with quantitative values ranging from *all* (*76%–100%*), *most* (*51%–75%*), *some* (*26%–50%*), and *few* (*1%–25%*) to *none* (0) were created for purposes of evaluation. In this section, we report on a few of the more salient findings related to the usefulness of the framework, based on responses from four senior managers involved in the process.

First, one of the key advantages of the mapping framework is to ensure that data sources needed for important key decisions are available and well maintained. However, once the modeling has been done, the system provides for rapid adaptation. Consider, for example, that despite all of the excitement around Big Data, government organizations still experience significant barriers in accessing and curating data (Kim et al., 2014). This is not to say that these organizations do not have access to data. In many cases, the opposite might be true. They have too much data coming from disparate data sources. Trying to determine what is important and what is not can be a challenge. In addition, as goals change, or the priorities associated with certain goals change, the IS needs to adapt in order to reflect changes in the business context.

Accordingly, one of the important questions asked was the degree to which the framework enables the organization to recognize internal variability and diversity. Figure 9.6 shows results of the four senior managers interviewed, indicating that, in fact, the system could help anticipate most changes related to variability within the organization.

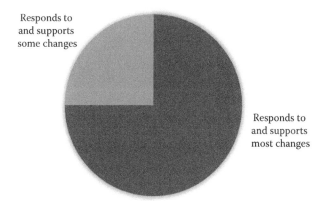

There was no responses to the framework for "responds to and supports all changes", responds to and supports few changes" and "responds to and supports no change"

Figure 9.6   Usefulness of framework for responding to diversity and variability within the organization.

Another key element in adaptation within large complex organizations is the ability to document changes such that an evolutionary trail is available to managers. The framework, because it is supported by software that records different snapshots in time of the IS, task/decisions, and business goals' linkages, provides a valuable means for documenting changes across the organization. Figure 9.7 shows the results of interviews with the four senior managers.

Finally, one of the key contributions of the framework is to align IS capabilities with business decisions and therefore business goals.

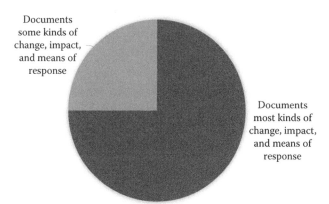

There was no responses to the framework for "documents all kinds of change, impact and means of response," "documents few kinds of change, impact and means of response" and "documents no kinds of change, impact and means of response."

Figure 9.7   Usefulness of framework for documenting change.

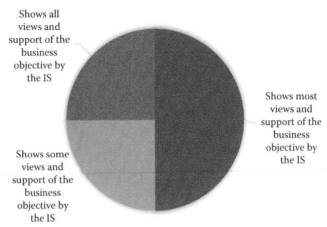

Shows all views and support of the business objective by the IS

Shows most views and support of the business objective by the IS

Shows some views and support of the business objective by the IS

There was no responses to the framework for "shows few views and support of the business objective by the IS" and "shows no views and support of the business objective by the IS"

Figure 9.8   Usefulness of framework for promoting business–information system alignment.

Figure 9.8 provides results of interviews with the four senior managers related to the framework's ability to align IS with business objectives.

Discussion and Conclusions

Government organizations cannot make use of Big Data if managers and analysts are overwhelmed by the available data or if they cannot make sense of the data. Sensemaking in this case has to occur within the context of business goals and the decisions that drive goal attainment. Linking data sources to business goals seems to be an obvious approach to ensuring that the data needed are available.

More importantly, organizations are not static, and public-sector organizations are noted for their relative complexity. Moreover, operational changes tend to be a feature of life in these organizations, since elections tend to introduce new policy frameworks and new programs. Therefore, adaptation is important, and frameworks that enable managers to add, delete, or modify ISs, as needed, support emerging policy priorities. The framework permits scenario analysis of all elements, such that the impact on satisfaction levels of deleting a data source can be estimated. In addition, if the quality of data source is changed, an assessment of the impact on satisfaction levels is automatically calculated.

Gupta and George (2016) suggest that building organizational capability for Big Data calls for a combination of technical and human resources. They further argue that until now, most of the emphasis has been on the technical aspects. In addition, data should be used to advance business goals through enhancing decision-making effectiveness of actors involved in carrying out tasks. However, it has been argued that the ways in which the use of Big Data influences decision making have not been well researched (Cao et al., 2015). These problems can be addressed if organizations, particularly those in the public sector, are able to define the ways in which specific ISs support specific business goals. Managers and analysts would then be in a better position to define the types of human skillsets needed to execute tasks supported by relevant data sources.

The modeling framework discussed in this paper provides a visual depiction of data sources that support specific organizational goals. Moreover, the linkages between and among the data sources, tasks to be done, and goals related to those tasks are also explicitly modeled. The managers in this organization found that the system provided a useful means of identifying change requirements and helped in better linking ISs to business goals. In a Big Data world, effective data management is crucial. However, it is difficult to manage data well without having a good understanding of the value of the data sources being developed or maintained.

References

Amyot, D. and Mussbacher, G. (2011). User requirements notation: The first ten years, the next ten years. *Journal of Software*, 6(5), 747–768.

Amyot, D., Shamsaei, A., Kealey, J., Tremblay, E., Miga, A., Mussbacher, G., Alhaj, M., Tawhid, R., Braun, E., and Cartwright, N. (2012). Towards advanced goal model analysis with jUCMNav. In S. Castano, P. Vassiliadis, L. V. S. Lakshmanan, and M. L. Lee (eds.), *ER Workshops 2012, LNCS*, vol. 7518, pp. 201–210. Berlin, Germany: Springer.

Cao, G., Duan, Y., and Li, G. (2015). Linking business analytics to decision making effectiveness: A path model analysis. *IEEE Transactions on Engineering Management*, 62(3), 384–395.

DeLone, W. and McLean, E. (2002). Information systems success revisited. *Proceedings of the 35th Annual Hawaii International Conference on System Sciences, HICSS*, IEEE CS, pp. 2966–2976.

DeLone, W. H. and McLean, E. R. (2003). The DeLone and McLean model of information systems success: A ten-year update. *Journal of Management Information Systems*, 19, 9–30.

Gupta, M. and George, J. F. (2016). Toward the development of big data analytics capability. *Information and Management*, 53, 1049–1064.

Hoogervorst, J. (2004). Enterprise architecture: Enabling integration, agility and change. *International Journal of Cooperative Information Systems*, 13, 213–233.

Kim, G.-H., Trimi, S., and Chung, J.-H. (2014). Big-data applications in the government sector. *Communications of the ACM*, 57(3), 78–85.

Mussbacher, G. and Amyot, D. (2009). Goal and scenario modeling, analysis, and transformation with jUCMNav. In *31st International Conference on Software Engineering - Companion Volume*, May 16–24, IEEE CS, pp. 431–432.

Saaty, T. L. (1988). *What is the Analytic Hierarchy Process?* Berlin, Germany: Springer, pp. 109–121.

Saaty, T. L. (1990). How to make a decision: The analytic hierarchy process. *European Journal of Operational Research*, 48(1), 9–26.

Yu, E., Deng, S., and Sasmal, D. (2012). Enterprise architecture for the adaptive enterprise - A vision paper. In S. Aier, M. Ekstedt, F. Matthes, E. Proper and J. L. C. Sanz (eds.), *TEAR/PRET*, pp. 146–161. Berlin, Germany: Springer.

10

ANALYZING PREDICTORS OF SEVERE TRAFFIC ACCIDENTS

SEAN GEDDES AND KEVIN LAI

Contents

Introduction

Predicting traffic collisions can be a daunting task because of the involvement of human factors and a large number of variables. To ensure clarity in our analysis, we followed a standardized framework known as Cross-Industry Standard Process for Data Mining (CRISP-DM).[1] The CRISP-DM framework consists of six clearly defined phases that encompass a data mining project. These phases include the following:

Phase 1: Business understanding
Phase 2: Data understanding
Phase 3: Data preparation
Phase 4: Modeling
Phase 5: Evaluation
Phase 6: Deployment

Phase 1: Business Understanding

The key business question being addressed was, *can we reliably model traffic collision data to predict severe traffic collisions based on the available data set and selected attributes?*

To address this question, techniques related to each phase of the CRISP-DM framework were applied, as discussed in the following:

1. *Data understanding*
   a. Basic statistics of variables, using a combination of RapidMiner, SPSS Modeler, and Excel.
   b. Using Python scripts to identify *zeros*, missing values, and unknowns.
2. *Data preparation*
   a. Clean data, using Python scripts.
   b. Format data for modeling, using Python scripts.
3. *Data modeling*
   a. Decision trees, using RapidMiner operators.
   b. Logistic regressions, using RapidMiner operators.
4. *Evaluation*
   a. Evaluate using performance operators in RapidMiner.
   b. Cross-validation methodology operators supplied by RapidMiner.
   c. Consider applicability of model results for the Ottawa police services (OPS).

Phase 2: Data Understanding

The initial data set used for this analysis is a confidential file protected by the Municipal Freedom of Information and Protection of Privacy Act (MFIPPA) and is titled *Collisions_2013*. This data set contains driver/vehicle collisions reported by the city's police services (in 2013). Since we were not involved in the original data collection, we made the assumptions that the data we obtained were accurate, relevant, consistent, and reliable.

The data set contained a total of 13,269 collisions involving 24,355 drivers/vehicles. It is important to note that there was no single unique identifier for the data set. The column *Accident ID* in Figure 10.1 is not a unique identifier for each record; instead, it represents a multi-vehicle

Column Name	Data Type
AccidentID	Integer
Date	Polynominal
Time	Polynominal
DayOfTheWeek	Polynominal
ACCIDENTLOCATION	Polynominal
Environment1	Polynominal
Light	Polynominal
TrafficControl	Polynominal
TRAFFICCONTROLCONDITION	Polynominal
Road Condition	Polynominal
Road Surface Condition	Polynominal
Road Alignment	Polynominal
PAVEMENTMARKINGS	Polynominal
Vehicle Type	Polynominal
Vehicle Condition	Polynominal
Driver Action	Polynominal
Driver Condition	Polynominal
ClassificationofAccident	Polynominal
Initial Direction of Travel	Polynominal
ImpactType	Polynominal
Vehicle Manoeuvre	Polynominal
SEQUENCE1	Polynominal
OFFSET1	Polynominal
SEQUENCE2	Polynominal
OFFSET2	Polynominal
SEQUENCE3	Polynominal
OFFSET3	Polynominal
Vehicle Damage	Polynominal
STREET1	Polynominal
STREET2	Polynominal
STREET3	Polynominal
Vehicle #	Polynominal
Vehicle Province	Polynominal
Driver Gender	Polynominal
Driver Age	Polynominal
Driver Charged	Polynominal
FAILEDTOREMAIN	Polynominal
X	Real
Y	Real

Figure 10.1 Data types.

collision that has a row for each driver/vehicle involved in each collision. The data set contained 39 variables, 36 of which are *polynominal*
data types; this data type is specific to RapidMiner, which can work
with any type of categorical data. In addition, the remaining three
variables are composed of one integer and two real data types. Data
types in Figure 10.1 provide a summary of the available data.

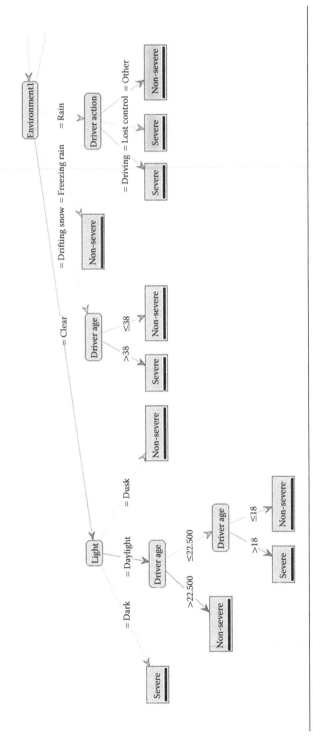

Figure 10.2   Decision Tree Model 1.

One of the issues is that many of the variables have *UNKNOWN*, *N/A*, or blank entries, as shown in Figure 10.2, unknown or missing data. We will return to this issue later in this report.

To gain a stronger understanding of the data, we investigated relative frequency counts of the values within the specific attribute headings. We sought to specifically investigate attributes that we deemed related to our *label* attributes: *severe* and *nonsevere* traffic collisions. The details of our inclusion and exclusion criteria, as well as our rationale, are described in detail in the data preparation section. As the data provided was in a *polynomial* format, this made quantifying basic statistical measures difficult (at least until the data had been cleansed and formatted). We decided that by determining the relative frequency of individual values corresponding to each attribute, we could identify interesting characteristics present in the data and develop a stronger understanding of the data set. The relative frequency and its absolute count for values corresponding to each attribute are as follows:

Regardless of the severity of the accident, there was not much variability in the fraction of traffic-accident occurrences on weekdays. The *Fraction* column in Table 10.1 shows that reported traffic accidents increase gradually throughout the week from Monday (0.136) to Friday (0.180). When looking at the weekend, it is interesting that the relative fraction is less than that in the weekdays, and the reported traffic-accident occurrences appeared to be twice as high on Saturdays when compared with Sundays (Table 10.1).

We found that the relative fraction of traffic accidents was highest in categories such as *intersection related*, *at intersection*, and *nonintersectional*. As the majority of drivers are more likely to be within these three categories while driving, we did not find this surprising. In addition,

Table 10.1 Frequency of Accidents by Day of the Week

INDEX	NOMINAL VALUE	ABSOLUTE COUNT	FRACTION
1	Friday	4395	0.180
2	Thursday	4246	0.174
3	Wednesday	3887	0.160
4	Tuesday	3741	0.154
5	Monday	3311	0.136
6	Saturday	2827	0.116
7	Sunday	1978	0.080

Table 10.2   Frequency of Accidents by Location

INDEX	NOMINAL VALUE	ABSOLUTE COUNT	FRACTION
1	Intersection related	8077	0.332
2	Non intersection	7550	0.310
3	At intersection	6115	0.251
4	At/near private drive	2441	0.100
5	Overpass or bridge	141	0.006
6	At railway crossing	25	0.001
7	Underpass or tunnel	6	0.000

when reporting the collision, it is possible that accidents can be easily grouped into these very general categories, resulting in a potential bias toward these obvious categories. We suspect that the data are valid for the location of the accident, but it is important to keep in mind that smaller subcategories that could have documented accidents at more specific locations might have been overlooked (Table 10.2).

When visualizing the driver's action attribute, we found it interesting that the majority of traffic collisions occurred when the driver was driving properly. This accounted for almost half of the relative fraction of traffic collisions when looking specifically at driver's action. One might expect this outcome when considering the documentation of multi-vehicle collisions. It is likely that at least one of the drivers (e.g., in a two-car collision) was driving properly and it was caused by another reckless

Table 10.3   Driver's Action

INDEX	NOMINAL VALUE	ABSOLUTE COUNT	FRACTION
1	Driving properly	11321	0.465
2	Failed to yield right-of-way	2287	0.094
3	Following too close	2285	0.094
4	Lost control	1870	0.077
5	Other	1499	0.062
6	Unknown	1037	0.043
7	Improper turn	969	0.040
8	Improper lane change	966	0.040
9	Speed too fast for condition	953	0.039
10	Disobeyed traffic control	741	0.030
11	Improper passing	323	0.013
12	Exceeding speed limit	68	0.003
13	Speed too slow	20	0.001
14	Wrong way on one-way road	16	0.001

Table 10.4 Frequency of Accidents and Driver's Condition

INDEX	NOMINAL VALUE	ABSOLUTE COUNT	FRACTION
1	Normal	16160	0.664
2	Inattentive	5626	0.231
3	Unknown	2063	0.085
4	Ability impaired, alcohol (over 0.8)	119	0.005
5	Fatigue	89	0.004
6	Other	88	0.004
7	Medical or physical...	82	0.003
8	Had been drinking	75	0.003
9	Ability impaired, alcohol (under 0.8)	44	0.002
10	Ability impaired, drugs	9	0.000

driver, who would fall in one of the other subcategories. In addition, it would be important to consider weather in relation to driver's action. For example, perhaps, the driver was driving properly, but there was still an accident due to poor road conditions, which could not be controlled.

Driver's age was another variable that we considered. The salient point is that after the age of 37 years, we found a gradual reduction in the number of accidents. This could be due to (1) a reduction in the number of drivers older than 37 years, and/or (2) driving experience levels for people older than 37 years.

Driver's condition was an important variable in that it could lead directly to accidents. Table 10.4 shows the distribution of accidents based on driver's condition. A large percentage of accidents occurred under conditions where the driver was considered *normal*, that is, not fatigued or intoxicated.

There were several other attributes examined, such as driver's gender, environment, time of day (related to daytime, evening, or nighttime), road condition, and pavement markings. Examination of these attributes allowed us to further clean the data and identify 15 key attributes important for the analysis.

Phase 3: Data Preparation

Initial Cleansing   We were able to decide on which attributes to select, based on understanding the attribute (and their values) in the previous sections, data availability, and relevance. Since metadata was not available, some attributes were removed to enable better understanding of the analysis.

As mentioned previously, the data set contained many *UNKNOWN*, *N/A*, and blank entries. A Python script was developed to deal with the *UNKNOWN* and *N/A* entries. Depending on the attribute, the script allocates a value to the *UNKNOWN*, *N/A*, and *other* values, which allowed the analytical tools to easily model the data, without outputting inaccurate results. By adding the default value, we will be able to quickly eyeball the software outputs and determine whether the *UNKNOWN* or *N/A* is significant to the analysis. We decided that by working with the data in this manner, instead of deleting the rows with *UNKNOWN* and *N/A*, we were able to maintain a significant amount of data, which would otherwise be removed.

Final Cleansing   When we began modeling the data, we found that previously assumed important attributes were unusable, because the context of the data was not compatible with our models. An example would be *FAILEDTOREMAIN*. This attribute's value is a *yes* if a driver failed to remain at the scene of the accident and a *no* if the driver remained at the scene of the accident. This was an event that happened after an accident and would obviously not be able to predict a severe accident. Another example would be *AccidentID*. Although this attribute would be beneficial for data querying, it is unusable in running our models, as the values have no meaningful representation.

In addition, to further simplify the data set, we decided to group the data from attribute *Vehicle Damage* from the five defined value groups (none, light, moderate, severe, and demolished) into only two groups for the analysis, *nonsevere*, containing data with *none*, *light*, and *moderate*, and *severe* containing *severe* and *demolished*, as the goal of the analysis is to find attributes that predict severe collisions. After many iterations, with a lot of trial and error, we determined that the optimal set of attributes for our models was as shown in Table 10.5.

Phase 4: Data Modeling

From our analysis of the data, we determined that decision trees and logistic regression models would be most useful in exploring the business question expressed earlier: Can we reliably model traffic collision data to predict severe traffic collisions based on our data set

Table 10.5 Final Attributes Used in the Analysis

ACCIDENT LOCATION
Day of the Week
Driver action
Driver age
Driver condition
Driver gender
Environment1
ImpactType
PAVEMENT MARKINGS
Road condition
Road surface condition
Traffic control
Vehicle condition
Vehicle damage

and selected attributes? In this section, we will discuss in depth the approach that we have taken to implement each model.

Decision Tree   Decision trees are one of the most widely used and practical methods for inductive inference.[2] We decided to use this approach in our initial modeling because of its ability to approximate discrete attributes found in the data set.

We began by designing a RapidMiner process; the first thing we did was to select the attributes, discussed earlier, from the data set. Within the decision tree node, we selected the "information_gain" criterion because of its ability to measure entropy, which is quantifying uncertainty associated with random variables. By determining entropy, the software will split a node based on attributes with minimum entropy. We felt that a confidence of 0.25 and minimal gain of 0.055 were the optimal values for our data, as they produced the most accurate model and the optimal tree size to derive meaningful insights. Because of the large data set, the breadth of the decision tree output was extremely complex. However, by examining subsets, certain insights were identified. As seen in the subset of the tree diagram, on rainy Fridays, there were the same amounts of severe collisions from vehicles approaching each other by drivers who were driving properly and by drivers who lost control.

More interestingly, the decision tree shows that on Fridays, drivers between the age of 18 years and 23 years who are driving in the day with clear weather are more susceptible to getting into a severe accident compared with drivers older than 38 years driving in drifting snow. Therefore, it seems as though age is a more significant attribute than weather when looking at severe collisions.

Figure 10.2 shows the impact of environment, light, and driver's age on the relative occurrence of severe and non-severe accidents.

From looking at collisions in the subset, Figure 10.3 shows that on Thursdays, with no traffic control (i.e., lights and signs):

- When pavement markings are obscured, there is a high outcome of collisions in snow with drivers younger than 40 years, compared with drivers older than 40 years.
- There is also a high outcome of severe collisions when there is drifting snow.
- When pavement markings do exist in the daylight, severe collisions occur mostly to drivers older than 51 years.

This subset of the tree shows us that having pavement markings on the roads with daylight does not matter, even if there were no traffic controls. Factors that affect severe collisions in this instance would be attributed to age and, potentially, snow.

Additional insights generated by the decision trees, as seen in the subset of decision tree to the right, when drivers got into a severe collision by losing control of their vehicles, the model tells us that it would happen mostly on a rainy Thursday. This fact maybe useful to the city's police service to help determine the factors contributing to severe collisions on Thursdays and to explore what they could do to mitigate these factors.

A cross-validation was conducted to evaluate the decision tree model; the output can be seen later. Despite extensive optimization of our model's parameters, the accuracy of our model is about 85.72%. Unfortunately, it has high accuracy only at predicting non-severe collisions. Not enough data were available to improve accuracy for severe collisions. These results may indicate that additional attributes are required to determine collision severity with decision tree models.

Logistic Regression Model   Logistic regression model is a commonly used model for measuring the relationship between categorical dependent and independent variables.[3] Based on previous studies on traffic

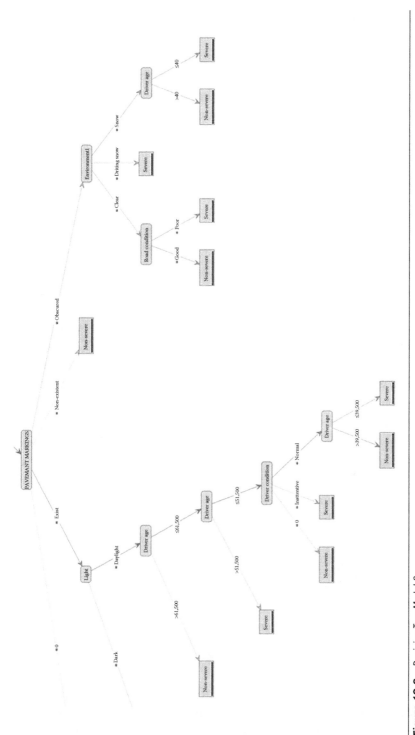

Figure 10.3 Decision Tree Model 2.

collisions and our extensive review of the literature, we determined that a logistic regression model maybe best suited for modeling this data set.[4,5] In this situation, as logistic regression models expect the target (or label) variable to be binary, we have set our dependent variable as a binary option by designating severe and non-severe traffic collisions as our label function (similar to as mentioned above). In addition, it is expected that the independent variables will be numeric, and this was readily accomplished by using our Python script to assign numeric values to categorical values related to each attribute.

We partitioned the data to designate a portion of the data to train the model and another portion of the data for testing. To accomplish this, we applied a split data operator and applied a 70/30 split in the data for training/testing. This 70/30 split was determined based on previous studies and generally accepted practices. Finally, we used a *performance classification* operator to assess performance of the logistic regression model. We were then ready to *run* the model.

When predicting the occurrence of an event in a RapidMiner logistic regression model, the tool automatically sets the cut-off probability to 0.5. This value essentially means that if the confidence of predicting a severe accident is more than 0.5, it will be deemed an accurate prediction. As a first test, we wanted to determine the performance of our model with this default parameter of 0.5 confidence. Our results revealed an overall accuracy of the model of 75.6%. Despite the high accuracy of the overall model, when specifically looking at the prediction of severe accidents, there was a relatively low accuracy of ~20%. This same model revealed ~80% success in predicting non-severe traffic collisions. As we were specifically interested in the ability of this model to predict *severe* accidents, we shifted the parameter settings to have a 0.85 cut-off confidence. This decision was based on the following:

1. Previous studies attempting to isolate the prediction of one of the binary events as labels.[6]
2. The higher weight of the non-severe class of the data set has the ability to drastically drop the accuracy of the severe class.

By raising the threshold, this essentially changes the level of confidence that each class has to meet to be deemed a successful prediction. This thresholding essentially works in an inverse manner by applying a stricter criterion for one class to be successfully predicted (higher cut-off) and a more moderate criterion for the other class to be predicted (lower cut-off). To implement this *threshold*, we used two threshold operators, as made evident by the following process image (Create and Apply Threshold). Following the use of this new threshold, we ran the model once again.

The performance vector yielded an 80.2% accuracy in predicting severe accidents when the threshold was set to 0.85. Despite the overall model having a lower accuracy of 44.21%, we were strictly interested in determining whether it could successfully predict severe accidents. Our readings indicated that this is a commonly used practice in business when you are interested in isolating one of your binary label pairs.

To further observe the effect of adjusting the threshold, we changed the threshold once again from 0.85 to 0.95. Expectedly, we were able to see a drastic increase in the accuracy of predicting severe accidents with the application of this new threshold.

Using a logistic regression model with binary classes of severe and non-severe classes yielded interesting results in terms of the prediction of severe traffic collisions. We found that by partitioning the data into 70% (for training) and 30% (for testing), with a threshold confidence of 0.85, we were able to observe an 80.20% success in predicting the occurrence of severe accidents. It is important to note that despite the low level of accuracy of the entire model (44.21%), it is still valid to consider the successful prediction of the severe class. This model presented more convincing results than observed with the decision tree model presented previously.

Phase 5: Review Process

In this study, we investigated the appropriateness of decision tree and logistic regression models in successfully predicting severe and non-severe traffic accidents. With the attributes included in our decision tree model, we were unable to achieve substantial accuracy in predicting severe traffic collisions. However, the logistic regression model generated stronger accuracies in predicting our *label (or target)* variables. Despite having an overall accuracy of 44.21% in our logistic regression model, applying a 0.85 threshold enabled us to elevate our accuracy in predicting severe traffic collisions to 80.20%. We were able to further increase this accuracy by thresholding at a level of 0.95. For the purpose of this study, our goal was to yield an accuracy of more than 80% in predicting severe collisions. Therefore, we found the results from a 0.85 threshold to be satisfactory.

The analysis provides a baseline for additional study on this topic. We would first recommend creating a data dictionary for the data set. By having a better understanding of the data, analysts would be able to draw stronger insights from the data set, without any guessing or uncertainty. In addition, with proper metadata, analysts can more efficiently classify and organize the data set. By doing so, they would be able to integrate third-party data sets (e.g., to compare different cities or different years), without negatively affecting the integrity of the original data or the analysis.

Second, we recommend conducting spatial analysis using the X and Y coordinates and collision intersections represented by street names, which are all attributes in the data set, to map out collisions based on geographical locations in Ottawa. One method that we recommend would be to map all the coordinates through the Google Maps API and use the analytical utilities to determine the parts of Ottawa that contains the highest amount of severe collisions. By creating a visualization of the geographical data, analysts will have a clear, visual understanding of the data and would be able to drill down to a certain zone to determine what attributes in the area are causing collisions or determine whether further data collection is required to answer any unknowns.

Third, as our model yielded relatively low accuracies overall, it may prove to be beneficial to reassess the attributes used in our analysis. In re-evaluating our current attributes used, it maybe better to attempt to remove attributes that have highly biased distributions in frequency counts toward a single nominal value within the attribute of interest. Per the results and review process used in this study, the overall accuracy is too low to provide concrete conclusions. However, a number of key factors were identified for both the data and the analytic process, which would enable more accurate predictive analyses.

References

1. Piatetsky, G. 2016. CRISP-DM, still the top methodology for analytics, data mining, or data science projects. *Kdnuggetscom*. Available at: http://www.kdnuggets.com/2014/10/crisp-dm-top-methodology-analytics-data-mining-data-science-projects.html. Accessed December 22, 2016.
2. Decision tree learning. 2016. Available at: https://www.cs.princeton.edu/courses/archive/spring07/cos424/papers/mitchell-dectrees.pdf. Accessed December 22, 2016.
3. Statistics Solutions. Accessible at: http://www.statisticssolutions.com/what-is-logistic-regression/. Accessed December 21, 2016.
4. Al-Ghamdi, A. 2002. Using logistic regression to estimate the influence of accident factors on accident severity. *Accident Analysis and Prevention*, 34, 729–741.
5. Karacasu, M., Ergül, B., and Altin Yavuz, A. 2014. Estimating the causes of traffic accidents using logistic regresson and discriminant analysis. *International Journal of Injury Control and Safety Promotion*, 21, 305–313.
6. Stack Exchange: Cross Validated. Accessible at: http://stats.stackexchange.com/questions/25389/obtaining-predicted-values-y-1-or-0-from-a-logistic-regression-model-fit. Accessed December 21, 2016.

Epilogue

An Analytic Maturity Model for Government Organizations

Maturity models are common in the field of business intelligence and analytics. They are often created to identify stages along a path of capability within specific domains. Most models are based on the Capability Maturity Model, initially conceived for the software development process. All these models include a process framework along with some form of assessment, indicating where an entity is situated along the path toward maturity.

Many such models are available for business intelligence maturity (Rajteric, 2010). Within the information systems literature, more than 130 models exist, and more recently, 14 maturity models specific to business analytics (BA) have been developed (Cosic, Shanks, & Maynard, 2012). Although none of these addresses public management, some e-government maturity models are available.

Maturity models can be developed for different purposes. For example, models can be descriptive, comparative, or prescriptive (de Bruin & Freeze, 2009). They may also operate in different ways—staged, continuous, or contextual. A staged model is sequential in that a lower stage must be completed before a subsequent stage. Continuous models recognize that the different stages might mature at different rates, thus providing a variety of paths to achieve maturity. Contextual models similarly permit different components within the model to evolve in different directions, thus providing a non-linear approach to maturity (Cosic et al., 2012).

Development of a maturity model calls for clarification of scope and domain, as well as a framing of how the model is to be used (de Bruin & Freeze, 2009). Given the paucity of such models for public management, what follows is a short review of a few existing BA maturity models and then articulation of a proposed government analytics maturity model.

Big Data Maturity Model of the Transforming Data with Intelligence (TDWI) includes 50 questions in five categories that include organization, infrastructure, data management, analytics, and governance. The model is staged in that organizations will progress from level 1 (nascent) to level 5 (mature/visionary) (Halper & Krishan, 2013). The view from IBM shows a similar staged process, during which organizations build their analytics quotient from novice through to master (Boyer et al., 2012). Tom Davenport's and Jeanne Harris's DELTA model encompasses five components: data, enterprise orientation, leadership, targets, and analysts (Davenport & Harris, 2010). By assessing these five components, organizations may progress from level 1 (analytically impaired) through to level 5 (analytical competitor).

Common components of all these models include access to data; therefore, data management is important. Governance and leadership are also critical issues, because without a culture that values evidence-based decision making, the analytics effort would be wasted. It is also important that the organization has access to analytics talent. This is not to say that all organizations need to hire data scientists, but each should have access to analytics talent in some form if they are to make sense of the available data.

The literature provides guidance in assessing the scope of such models for public management. The key question to be addressed is what really is the role of BA within organizations. Holsapple, Lee-Post, and Pakath (2014) identify three different traditions that describe the activities and outputs related to analytics. The first tradition focuses on activities: describe, prescribe, and predict. The second tradition addresses the outputs of analytics: sensing, predictions, evaluations, and decisions. The third one highlights organizational impact that includes agility, innovation, and reputation. A clear progression can be noted among these three traditions in that analytics generates insights that lead to positive organizational impact.

This sequence of events: analytic activities, outputs, and organizational impact, has been considered from the viewpoint of information processing theory (Cao, Duan, & Li, 2015; Kowalczyk & Buxmann, 2014). Viewed from this perspective, the overall contribution of analytics is to reduce uncertainty, thus enabling decisions that lead to program effectiveness or efficiency. This means that change is implied in the use of analytics. If all we do is analyze, but no operational changes are put in place, why bother analyzing data at all? Therefore, one of the key elements missing from BA maturity models is this notion of sharing of results and/or some form of integrated change management process.

Research into organizational analytics capability also provides a framework for scoping of a BA maturity model. In a comprehensive review of the field along with surveys of more than 200 Big Data and Analytics professionals (Gupta & George, 2016), key factors that lead to analytics capability were defined as tangible resources (data, technology, and basic resources), human resources (managerial and technical skills), and intangible resources (data-driven culture and intensity of organizational learning).

Based on the foregoing and current research into the use of analytics and performance measures in public-sector organizations, the following appear to be the key components of government analytics maturity model:

1. Governance and leadership specific to the use of Big Data and Analytics.
2. A well-developed supply chain.
3. An analytics service model.
4. Methods in place to disseminate learning from analytics and to support change.

Governance and Leadership

Every maturity model will address governance and leadership. In public-sector organizations, the important point is that senior leadership focuses attention on the use of analytics to drive resource allocation and operational improvement decisions. For example, in one organization studied for the purposes of this paper, the head of the organization—once the BA tools were in place—insisted that every presentation for budget allocation or for new ways of working be accompanied by a sound analysis based on available data. Another organization defined the flow of analysis as: from the front lines, through regional management, to executive management. The idea is that each report was vetted by those closest to the action. By the time the reports reached senior management, improvement ideas were already noted and supported by the data, and decision rights had been clarified. That is, everyone in the management network knew who had the authority to make decisions about what.

The point is that senior leaders in these organizations treated data as an asset important to accomplishment of organizational goals and ensured to the degree possible that the asset was being used effectively for decision making. Clearly, senior managers have many other things to do. What was noted in these organizations was that, despite the busy workloads of the senior leadership team, they visibly paid attention to how data were being used.

A final point is that within public-sector organizations, senior leadership tends to change regularly. Accordingly, organizations using data well find a way to institutionalize analytics within their budgeting and process improvement processes. It becomes a way of doing business and is not considered a *bolt-on* to regular organizational tasks.

A Well-Developed Supply Chain

All BA maturity models discuss the importance of data. In those public-sector organizations that I have studied this far, none suffered from a lack of data. In fact, most had so much data available that their challenge was more about deciding what was important. Therefore, the idea of a data supply chain that transforms and delivers *relevant* data to decision makers appeared to be more important than access to data itself. Moreover, within the data supply chain, a degree of *data discipline* existed. This meant that common definitions of key data points existed and managers relied on centralized, validated data instead of creating separate data sources across the organization.

A Well-Developed Analytics Service Model

Organizations will need staff who can analyze data appropriately and work with program managers to extract meaning for program delivery. This is not to say that each organization needs to hire data scientists. Many public-sector organizations partner with universities or other analytics service providers, when needed. The point here is that analytics services are available for both analysis and interpretation, and program managers know how to access these services. Furthermore, external data in the form of benchmarks or objective reviews of findings are used, where necessary, to provide assurance of the accuracy and meaningfulness of the analysis. This is an important element in triggering the change process that often follows the analytics process.

Methods in Place to Disseminate and Apply Lessons Learned

In those organizations that used BA well, senior management made it clear that analytics is in service of expected outcomes. Therefore, regular checkpoints exist on progress toward these outcomes, so that the analytics effort is seen as an investment in outcomes realization. In addition, lessons learned through analysis are disseminated widely throughout the organization. The idea is that since all organization members have a stake in outcome realization, all should have a stake in thinking through how to better meet these outcomes.

One key finding from some of the organizations that I have studied is that they explore potential courses of actions carefully before implementing change. Public-sector organizations operate in a fish bowl environment. In addition, many work with unions and other stakeholder groups; therefore, change processes need to be inclusive. To do so, proposed changes should be studied carefully and reviewed objectively before being implemented.

Finally, it is important to follow up on outputs of analytics-driven change processes. By assessing the impact on outcome realization of these change processes, the organization can learn from both successes and failures. Once again, transparency is important, so that all stakeholders are fully informed.

Summary

Figure 1 depicts the model discussed previously. The shaded boxes identify the four components, with arrows leading to the second-order effects of each of the components of the model. Given that public-sector organizations differ significantly in size, mandate, and the degree of risk involved in their operations, the model is more contextual than staged. That is, each of the four components could develop independently. For example, a large regionalized organization might have some regions that develop their analytic service model through the actions of program managers, without necessarily noting strong interest of the senior management team. Over time, senior management may notice the work being done in this region and seek to institutionalize these initiatives across the organization.

In addition, the model is meant to be descriptive, not prescriptive. Different public-sector organizations might find different ways of creating analytic service models, for example. The model does not suggest that analysts need to be internal to the organization. Clearly, those public-sector organizations that work in highly risky or secure domains might need internal analysts, while others might be able to contract out their analytics service requirements.

The proposed model is not meant to be exhaustive but rather to serve as a high-level assessment. It can be used at any level in the organization, and the assessment should be done by the responsibility manager (i.e., the program manager responsible for delivering results). Moreover, some of the existing maturity models (such as the comprehensive model developed by TDWI) might be used for a more detailed assessment, especially related to the data supply chain component of the model shown in Figure 1.

Further validation of the proposed maturity model will be required, but for the moment, recognizing the variety of public-sector organizations that exists and the fact that most of these organizations operate in an environment where transparency is important, this high-level model can be used to generate an initial assessment of analytics maturity.

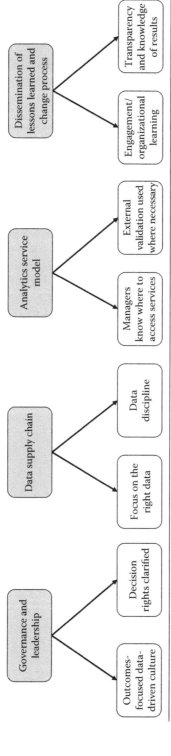

Figure 1 Proposed Government Analytics Maturity Model.

References

Boyer, J., Frank, B., Green, B., Harris, T., & Van De Vanter, K. (2012). *5 keys to business analytics success*. Boise, ID: MC Press.

Cao, G., Duan, Y., & Li, G. (2015). Linking business analytics to decision making effectiveness: A path model analysis. *IEEE Transactions on Engineering Management*, 62(3), 384–395.

Cosic, R., Shanks, G., & Maynard, S. (2012). *Towards a business analytics capability maturity model*. 23rd Australasian Conference on Information Systems, Geelong, Australia.

Davenport, T. H., & Harris, J. G. (2010). *Analytics at work: Smarter decisions better results*. Boston, MA: Harvard Business School Publishing.

de Bruin, T., & Freeze, R. (2009). *Understanding the main phases of developing a maturity assessment model*. 16th Australasian Conference on Information Systems, Sydney, Australia.

Gupta, M., & George, J. F. (2016). Toward the development of big data analytics capability. *Information & Management*, 53, 1049–1064.

Halper, F., & Krishan, K. (2013). *TDWI big data maturity model guide*. Renton, Washington: The Data Warehousing Institute.

Holsapple, C., Lee-Post, A., & Pakath, R. (2014). A unified foundation for business analytics. *Decision Support Systems*, 64, 130–141.

Kowalczyk, M., & Buxmann, P. (2014). Big data and information processing in organizational decision processes. *Business and Information Systems Engineering*, 5, 267–278.

Rajteric, I. H. (2010). Overview of business intelligence maturity models. *Management*, 15, 47–67.

Index